THE INDEPENDENT PUBLISHER

Other Books by Jerrold R. Jenkins

Publish to Win: Smart Strategies to Sell More Books

Inside the Bestsellers

THE INDEPENDENT PUBLISHER

How to Build and Promote Your Best-Selling Book

JERROLD R. JENKINS

with Jillian Bergsma

JENKINS GROUP
Traverse City, MI

© 2012 Jerrold R. Jenkins

All rights reserved. No part of this publication may be reproduced, stored in retrieval system, or transmitted in any form or by any means electronic, mechanical, photocopying, recording or otherwise, without the prior written permission of the publisher.

Published by
Jenkins Group, Inc.
Traverse City, Michigan
www.bookpublishing.com

Publisher's Cataloging-in-Publication Data
Jenkins, Jerrold R.

The independent publisher : how to build and promote your best-selling book / by Jerrold R. Jenkins, with Jillian Bergsma. – Traverse City, Mich. : Jenkins Group Inc., 2012.

p. ; cm.

ISBN13: 978-0-9860224-0-1

1. Small presses—United States. 2. Publishers and publishing—United States. 3. Best sellers. I. Title. II. Bergsma, Jillian.

Z231.5.L5 J46 2012
070.50973—dc23   2012947509

FIRST EDITION

Project coordination by Jenkins Group, Inc.
www.BookPublishing.com

Front cover design by Chris Rhoads
Interior design by Yvonne Fetig Roehler

Printed in the United States of America
16 15 14 13 12 • 5 4 3 2 1

To the writers and publishers that understand the need to build something better than a book. The people who know that it is necessary to create a valuable product, sell it at a reasonable price, and tie it together with perfect placement and effective promotion: in essence, the necessity to create a book business. And to all of those who have a love for writing that cannot be damaged by failure but will be satisfied only by success.

Contents

Acknowledgments ix
Introduction xi

1   The Freeman's Oath
    A Short History of Independent Publishing 1

SECTION I: PRODUCT AND PRICE

2   Ready to Kill Some Trees?
    Make Your Book Worth the Wood 15

3   A Great Title
    Grab Attention, Sell More Books 23

4   Setting the Foundation
    Realizing Your Editorial Needs 31

5   Designing Your Book
    Pretty Gets Noticed 41

6   E-Book Creation and Conversion
    A Companion Format to Physical Books 61

7   Priced to Sell
    What Should I Charge? 67

SECTION II: PLACE

8   Bookstores
    Are They Really the Worst Place to Sell Books? 77

9   Independent Publishers and Independent Booksellers
    Working Together? 89

10 Safely Navigating Amazon.com
    (and Other Online Booksellers) 93

11 Building Your Website
    Be Google Ready 101

12 PRINT-ON-DEMAND
   A WAY IN, NOT A WAY AROUND 109
13 BREAKING INTO INDIEBOUND
   "BOOK SENSE EVOLVED" 115
14 MANAGING THE MASS MARKET
   DISCOUNT OUTLETS 123

SECTION III: PROMOTION

15 DETERMINING YOUR MARKET
   WHO WANTS TO READ YOUR BOOK? 131
16 USING SOCIAL MEDIA
   BEYOND FACEBOOK 139
17 BOOK REVIEWS
   THE GOOD, THE BAD, THE PAID FOR 149
18 ADVERTISING AND SPECIAL SALES
   SELLING DIRECT TO CONSUMER 157
19 BOOK AWARDS AND BOOK CLUBS
   SHINY STICKERS, EXPOSURE, AND PRESTIGE 167
20 CATALOG SALES
   BIG ADVANTAGES OVER RETAIL SALES 173
21 DIRECT MARKETING
   BOOKS ARE A PERFECT PRODUCT FOR DIRECT MAIL 183
22 GIFT AND SPECIALTY STORES
   SELLING IN NONBOOK RETAIL STORES 191
23 ALTERNATIVE SALES PLATFORMS
   CORPORATIONS, ASSOCIATIONS, FOUNDATIONS,
   AND THE GOVERNMENT 199
   CONCLUSION
   THE FOUR PS REVISITED 211
   APPENDIX 213
   BIBLIOGRAPHY 217
   ABOUT THE AUTHOR 221

Acknowledgments

First, to Jillian Bergsma—this book would not have been possible without her efforts. Also, thanks to everyone at Jenkins Group who offered his or her time and contacts and to those who attended the way-too-long title meetings, water balloons and all.

There are too many people to thank in such a small place, but a few need mentioning: Steven Bollinger (without whom this book would have never been completed), Rebecca Chown, Jon Roth, Dan Prisciotta, Jenna McCarthy, Charles J. Orlando, W. Patrick Clarke, R. William Bennett, Marty Clarke, Judith M. Johnson, Tim Smith, Jim Denardo, Bev Harris, Adam Salomone, Chad W. Post, Patti Miller, and John Oakes.

Finally, a big thank-you to all of the authors, consultants, salespeople, and publishers who worked with us during this book. We appreciate your insights and your dedication to helping aspiring writers get good work out there.

Introduction

"Getting published is a combination of determination and luck."
—MARK BOWDEN, author of *Black Hawk Down: A Story of Modern War*

To tweak Bowden's quote for the twenty-first century, you might say that getting *published* is a combination of time and money but getting read is a combination of determination, luck, and a little bit more money. Almost anyone can be published (or, rather, can publish himself or herself), but only a very small percentage of that group has serious readership.

We writers all dream of publishing the next best seller in our genre, the enduring, universally acknowledged work of art that is beloved by literate folks the world over. How many people achieve this goal? Well, now we can actually say one in a million (or thereabouts). But being published, whether it is by a reputable publisher or a vanity press, is no guarantee of success.

With R.R. Bowker listing hundreds of thousands of new books per year, it's no secret that getting your book in print or online is a relatively simple task. But, as an author, part of the dream is selling some of those books, right? You want to capture readers who will fall in love with your writing, your characters, or your ideas. To put it simply, you can't get that kind of attention without working quite a bit harder than the next person.

The Independent Publisher was created with the hope of helping authors work that much harder. We wanted to give you the tools and tricks of the trade that will allow you to build your book into a polished and profitable good—not just a pretty book with a nice font and a flashy cover but a pretty book that will sell and be enjoyed by your potential readers. With twenty-five years as a leader in the custom-book-publishing business, Jenkins Group has had plenty of experience consulting, guiding, and working with authors who are looking to produce a book. There are millions of book titles available to the public these days, and it's important that your book stands out.

When we started writing the book, Jim Kalajian, president and COO here at Jenkins Group, told me that the only thing (I exaggerate) that he remembered from his college years was the marketing rule of the four Ps. For those of you unfamiliar with the concept, the four Ps—product, price, place, and promotion—were introduced in the 1960s by Michigan State University Professor E. Jerome McCarthy. As a whole, they represent the start-to-finish steps to put a valuable book out on the market. We decided to theme our book around these principles and give writers a comprehensive guide to writing, publishing, and selling their books.

We'll bet that when you began putting your story into words, you thought that your job title would be limited to "author" and wouldn't include "marketing director," "headhunter," or "sales manager." This myth came from the authors who get picked up by the Big Six. They have little to fear when it comes to their work because the giant corporate houses know it's their job to make a book sell. However, if you're self-publishing or working with a smaller house, some of the decisions and obligations will fall to you. We'll walk you through determining your market, steer you away from editorial and design faux pas, and give you tips on how to price your book and where to sell it.

As brick-and-mortar mega-bookstores seem to be losing ground, finding an alternative sales platform is essential to the success of your book. Knowing the ins and outs of Amazon.com, corporations, and direct marketing campaigns can help enlarge your audience and increase your sales. In addition, because the Internet has become the be-all and end-all in today's market, *The Independent Publisher*

Introduction

will give you helpful hints when it comes to creating your website and will present social media success stories and shortcuts that will make your book take off.

I'll give our most important takeaway point here in the intro (consider it a bonus point for not skipping these first few pages): professional work is key. By this we mean that working with a pro, from manuscript to sales to your public persona, is the only way to go. I'm talking about using an editor, working with an interior designer, hiring a web developer, consulting with a PR rep—the list goes on. If I had my way, I'd ask Mr. McCarthy to add "professional" as the fifth P. Creating and selling a professional book isn't difficult, and it doesn't have to be expensive. But having a well-made book, an easy-to-navigate website, and a series of different channels through which to sell your work will set you apart from the publishing masses.

Building your book is like building a house: you start with the foundation (the edited manuscript), put the walls in place (exterior design), decorate (interior design), and add any special touches of your own. Then there are all those trade standards that your house must meet and inspectors who have to give you the go-ahead or else shut you down. (By the way, those standards are set by companies such as Random House, Wiley, and Simon & Schuster, and those inspectors are readers, bookstore owners, librarians, and critics.) At the end of the day, you want to have used your money wisely and have built a house that guests will enjoy and that—somewhere down the road—someone will buy.

The thing is you'd hire someone to do almost every step of this process, right? Very few people are qualified to build their own house, and it's one thing you really don't want to screw up. The same goes for your book. While you can write it (or hire a ghostwriter with ease), you probably can't publish it and market it and get the audience you want without a bit of professional help.

The web (and the phone book, if you still have one) is full of companies and individuals who can help you along your path to publishing greatness. Our hint? Treat every potential editor, designer, and rep like a potential contractor. Just as you wouldn't let a used-car salesperson build your home, don't let just anybody take care of your book. Conduct interviews, ask for recommendations or samples of work, and, above all, use your best judgment.

The Independent Publisher uses the four Ps, expert advice, and Jenkins Group's decades of experience in the business to give you a leg up on your competitors out there. We're not promising you'll be the next Amanda Hocking, but there's a good chance that taking our advice will increase your readership from your closest friends and family to some of those nice, literature-hungry strangers out there: the folks who need your advice, stories, or insight, even if they don't know it just yet—the people you wanted to reach in the first place.

"The profession of book writing makes horse racing seem like a solid, stable business."
—JOHN STEINBECK

THE FREEMAN'S OATH

A Short History of Independent Publishing

It seems fitting that, as far as historians know, the first document ever published in the United States was published by an independent publisher. While the early stages of corporate hierarchy and top-down decision making were beginning to be felt in the publishing markets of Europe by the fifteenth century, the liberty-minded (and financially constrained) American colonists would have none of that. So, for readers who think that independent, small-press, self-, and mircopublishing are new phenomena, think again.

The very first piece of writing ever to be mass-produced in the United States was titled, appropriately enough, *The Oath of a Freeman*. It was printed in 1639 by Stephen Daye in a printing shop set up at Harvard University (then called Harvard College) in Cambridge, Massachusetts. Daye was not a writer, or an editor, or a bookseller, but rather a printing technician—which means he had ink stains on his fingers and knew how to set up, run, and fix a printing press. He had sailed to Cambridge from England with his employers, the Reverend and Mrs. Jose Glover. When the reverend died on the journey, his wife and Daye set up the printing shop without him and tried out their cobbled-together press on the freeman pamphlet that invited Massachusetts's residents to swear their allegiance to their fledgling government. Some credit *The Oath of the Freeman* as one of the precursors of the Declaration of Independence, written (and subsequently published) more than 130 years later.

The Oath of a Freeman

I, being (by God's providence) an Inhabitant, and Freeman, within the jurisdiction of this Commonwealth, do freely acknowledge my self to be subject of the government thereof and therefore do here swear by the great and dreadful name of the Ever living God, that I will be true and faithful to the same and will accordingly yield assistance and support thereunto, with my person and estate, as in equity I am bound: and will also truly endeavor to maintain and preserve all the liberties and privileges thereof, submitting my self to the wholesome laws and orders made and stabilized by the same; and further, that I will not plot, nor practice any evil against it nor consent to any that shall so do, but will timely discover and reveal the same to lawful authority now here established, for the speedy preventing thereof. Moreover, I do solemnly bind myself, in the sight of God, that when I shall be called to give my voice touching any such matter of this state, (in which freemen are to deal) I will give my vote and suffrage as I shall judge in my own conscience my best conduct and tend to the public weal of the body, without respect of persons or favor of any man. So help me God in the Lord Jesus Christ.

The Freeman's Oath

The following year, Daye printed seventeen hundred copies of the *Bay Psalm Book*, eleven copies of which survive today and are scattered around the country in museums and private collections. Mrs. Glover died soon after the *Bay Psalm Book* was published (but not before marrying Harvard's first president, Henry Dunster). By 1640, the printing shop was formally named the Cambridge Press, and despite its rapid and tragic changes in leadership, it published a book a year for the next twenty-one years. Gives some historical authority to today's small publishers' book-a-year publishing programs, doesn't it?

Yes, the U.S. independent publishing industry, including—horrors!—self-publishers, can claim credit for disseminating some of the noblest writing ever published in this country. Walt Whitman first published his poetic masterpiece, *Leaves of Grass*, himself in 1855. Mark Twain took the same route with his classic tales of Southern American boyhood, *Adventures of Huckleberry Finn* and *The Adventures of Tom Sawyer*. Ben Franklin was a self-publisher, as was Thomas Paine. Other writers of note whose first work was either self-published or brought out by very small presses include Henry David Thoreau, Ernest Hemingway, Rudyard Kipling, e.e. cummings, Carl Sandberg, D. H. Lawrence, George Bernard Shaw, Beatrix Potter, Allen Ginsberg, Dorothy Allison, John Asbury, Julia Cameron, James Schuyler, John Grisham, and Sherman Alexie. Jenkins Group's first book, *Inside the Bestsellers*, contains the stories behind the successes of more contemporary self-published books, including *50 Simple Things You Can Do to Save the Earth*, *Love You Forever*, and *The Macintosh Bible*.

Ah, but how incomplete our bookshelves would be if only the most noble thoughts made it into print. And how hypocritical we would be if we didn't acknowledge that some—you might even say many—books published by self-publishers are, for lack of a better term, tree killers. Blame those liberty-minded colonists if you want to, because those same rebels who gave us democracy, and Thanksgiving, and popcorn also gave us freedom of speech. So, our nation's independent publishing industry can take credit for putting in front of readers not only the work of the most noble writers but also some of the more, shall we say, commonplace works. These include such self-published titles as *The Pleistocene Redemption* (of which an Amazon.com reviewer wrote that the book was "pulped and now mulching my wife's tomatoes"), and let's not forget Richard Nixon's *Real Peace: A Strategy for the West*, in which the former president, who is remembered today by many as a crook and a bungler, lays out his foreign policy theories in all their self-published glory.

I defer to one of our generation's consummate bookmen, Jason Epstein. "The gift of storytelling is uncommon," he writes in *Book Business*. "It can be seen at a glance even by a beginner like myself."

In their heart of hearts, publishers know this. Readers certainly do. Every single person may indeed have a book inside of him or her. Whether it should ever be let out, or whether these people should write and publish it themselves, is and should always be a personal decision (those colonists again). There is nothing in the First Amendment about hiring a good editor, but those who decide to publish—and you are probably one of them if you are reading this book—should keep foremost in their minds that the market will weigh in on the soundness of their decision. And the market always presses a fat thumb on the scale.

"The demands of the market have no ideology; they have been cleansed of it, they are pure, desirable, wreathed in glamour and glory," writes Dubravka Ugresic in her biting critique of the book industry, *Thank You for Not Reading*. "What the market decides is confirmed by millions, and its moral dimension is not in question."

It is that market that has dispassionately guided this most passionate of industries for the past 360-plus years. For example, it was the market that tempted even the most reputable American publishers in the mid-1800s to issue unauthorized reprints of successful English writers, even though those publishers, with names such as Charles Scribner and Fletcher Harper and Thomas Mosher, had to have known that the activity made them out to be little better than the pirates of the day. But then, when our own American-born writers began making names for themselves (and profits for their publishers) and were subsequently ripped off by foreign publishers reprinting their work without permission, it was the market that urged Congress to pass the International Copyright Act in 1891. Indirectly, it spurred the beginnings of many independent publishers, as the established, corporate publishers continued to work with only the most bankable authors, both British and American, such as Charles Dickens and James Fennimore Cooper, leaving available the more unknown, marginal, and experimental writers.

"Authors who experimented aesthetically or challenged the social status quo were judged immoral, radical, or economically unsound and so were rejected," writes Illinois State University English Professor Robert McLaughlin, who has researched the U.S. alternative and independent publishing industry. "As a result, an atmosphere developed in which ground-breaking work was ignored." Sound familiar? Well, don't be too quick to ally yourself with these literary mavericks of history.

Seeing an opportunity to publish the work of those "radical" authors, independent publishers with names such as Copeland, Day, Lamson, Wolffe & Co., Small, Maynard & Co., and R.H. Russell were founded, and through their efforts, Americans had their first opportunity to read new work, published domestically, by Oscar Wilde, W. B. Yeats, George Bernard Shaw, H.G. Wells, and Gabriel Rossetti. While those idealistic publishers are to be commended for their commitment to literature, they were completely noncommercial in both their philosophies and, unfortunately, their business practices. Their story is as much a cautionary tale as the contemporary plan to self-publish *Jesus Was an Alien*. You probably don't recognize their company names, despite the pedigree of their authors, because not one of those idealistic publishers survived the nineteenth century. Every one of them went bankrupt.

In one case, it was the market that dictated to publishers in the early to mid-1900s that if the purpose of books was intellectual stimulation, an elitist attitude for an elitist activity, then in order to appeal to this type of reader, books should be expensively made and expensively priced. Publishers of the day were putting out a product aimed at consumers much like themselves: white, educated, urban, and financially comfortable. But then came the end of World War II, the Marshall Plan, the G.I. Bill of Rights, and the beginnings of suburban migration coupled with rapid economic, industrial, and technological growth, as well as soaring printing costs. While the break-even point for a new hardcover book had been sales of approximately one thousand copies in the 1880s, by 1952 a publisher had to sell four to eight thousand copies to recoup its investment, according to McLaughlin. At the same time, a new generation of the working middle class wanted to turn to books for education, entertainment, and, yes, even intellectual stimulation. The market smiled on a brilliant innovation: the trade paperback. Dover Books, Anchor Books, Allen Lane's Penguins, Penguin Specials, Penguin Classics, King Penguins, and Puffin Books, along with independent publishing's Evergreen paperbacks from Grove Press and Quinn Publishing's Handi-Books, were cheap, lightweight, attractive, and entertaining.

Today, while corporate publishers usually still release their lead titles in hardcover first and follow with the trade and/or mass-market paperback version of the book, independent publishers oftentimes go straight to trade paperback to conserve capital and allow the book to be priced to appeal to a broader audience. This tactic has worked especially well, for example, for Workman Publishing. The large independent publisher is best known for its *What to Expect* series of books on pregnancy and child rearing, and the company's first title, *Yoga 28-Day Exercise Plan*, published in trade paperback in 1968, is now in its twenty-eighth printing. The Workman style of publishing could be used like a mantra of success for new and experienced independent publishers alike: "The bright, appealing trade-paperback format. High standards of design and production. Authors who are authorities, who tour extensively, and are spokespeople for their subjects. And above all, value through conscientious, aggressive pricing." Aggressive pricing has helped make

Workman titles a darling of retail bookstores, but as you'll see later in this book, the saying "Bookstores are the worst place to sell books" may be cliché in our industry, but that doesn't make it untrue, especially for the smallest publishers.

By the 1970s, when suburban migration was in its heyday and the shopping mall was becoming the town center for an increasing number of consumers, including readers, the mall bookstore had to contend with a market condition that the corner bookseller did not: exorbitant rents. While the traditional independent bookseller owned its own building, worked out long-term leases with its landlord, or operated in a corner of downtown where rent was affordable, books stocked in shopping mall storefronts had to generate the same profit per square foot as shoes, fast food, men's suits, and diamond jewelry. By the mid-1980s, when the sweet smell of Cinnabon rolls wafted through the mall for the first time, competing with McDonald's French fries and the spray of the Orange Julius mixing machine, B. Dalton and Waldenbooks bookstore chains were ravenous, day in and day out, for a diet of best sellers. Not a good fit for small publishers who not only didn't generate many but also continued to promote and depend on the sale of their title(s) long after they were considered "new books." This obsession with the new is a fact of retail bookselling that doesn't fit with our nostalgic image of the cozy book shoppe with its stock of esoteric literature and soft lighting, but it is a fact of the market, nonetheless.

By the 1990s, the independent bookstores that small, self-, and independent publishers had come to rely on to stock their books, host their authors for readings, and "hand-sell," or personally recommend their books to customers, were locked in a fight for their fiscal lives with Barnes & Noble, the mall bookstores, Walmart, and, by 1995, the Internet and Amazon.com.

Best-selling author Barbara Kingsolver (who is published by HarperCollins but still has her poetry published by Seal Press, an independent publisher) championed an independent bookstore, the Book Mark of Arizona, in an op-ed piece published in the

Arizona Daily Star. "I owe my career to people such as those at the Book Mark who first guided readers to my words. I think of them as family. When my daughter was born I sent them a birth announcement, which they proudly displayed. Yesterday, they sent me a much less joyful announcement: after 40 years, the Book Mark is passing away. Tucsonans' buying habits are changing: we now purchase through the Internet, we hunt for bargains, we're drawn by the lure of the chains."

In that op-ed piece, which was widely reprinted, Kingsolver expressed the feelings of many authors, as well as small publishers and, of course, independent booksellers. But all the nostalgia in the world couldn't compete with the market, and the large chains went through an exponential period of growth in the 1990s. In 1972, independent bookstores controlled 84 percent of the retail book market, according to an article by D. Kornhaber published in the Independent Online Booksellers Association (IOBA) Standard. By 1983, shortly after chain bookstores first began expanding, the independents' share fell to 71 percent, and by the end of the '90s, their market share had dropped to 15 percent. In addition, Barnes & Noble also now owns and operates the bookstores of more than six hundred colleges and universities.

Then came the era of big lawsuits. In her op-ed piece, Kingsolver not only lamented the closing of a favorite independent but also took the superstores to task for their business practices. "I have a bone to pick with the way the behemoth chains organize their bookselling," she wrote. "They don't play fair. They purposely out-compete the neighborhood shop, dazzling customers with glitzy displays and—above all—discounts. They can afford to cut the price of the latest blockbuster, because chains order these books by the thousands, at a reduced price that the publishers don't offer to the independents." The leaders of the Association of American Booksellers (ABA) agreed and had their attorneys file the requisite paperwork.

Beginning in May of 1994, the ABA began its Robinson-Patman Act litigation against several major publishers that the organization had charged were offering the superstore chains unfair and illegal trade terms. In March of 1998, the ABA went after the superstores directly. "All independent booksellers welcome honest competition from any facet of the industry," said ABA President Avin Mark Dominitz. "But because we believe that certain competitors have used their size and market clout to dominate the market to the detriment of the industry, we are waging this court battle, with the goal of securing a level playing field where all retailers obey the laws."

By the late 1990s, other book industry mainstays used the courts to help settle their disputes. Walmart sued Amazon.com in 1998, charging the Internet bookseller with hiring away employees in an effort to gain proprietary computer programming knowledge. Their official charge was that Amazon.com violated the Arkansas Trade Secrets Act. Also in 1998, Barnes & Noble announced plans to purchase Ingram Book Group, the nation's largest book wholesaler. Though no lawsuits were filed over the planned purchase, the ABA launched a letter-writing campaign that besieged the Federal Trade Commission with mail, arguing that the acquisition would provide Barnes & Noble with the buying patterns of independent booksellers and permit the superstore to delay shipment of sought-after books. Barnes & Noble denied the charges, but President Steve Riggio abandoned his company's plan to purchase the wholesaler in June of 1999, a day after numerous news outlets reported that the FTC wouldn't approve the deal.

Despite the relentless buildup of retail outlets that sell books, the past decade has been a challenging one for independent publishers. As a form of both entertainment and education, books compete not only with each other for readers—or "eyeballs" as industry commentators are fond of calling consumers—but also with myriad additional media. For decades, publishers were accustomed to the reality that their books competed with radio, television, and movies, but today you can add the iPad, Xbox, DVDs, smartphones, cable and satellite television, DVR, pay-per-view, and, of course, the Internet. A growing cottage industry operated through the Internet is the sale of used books. Some reports put the sale of used books on Amazon to be fully 20 percent of the online retailer's total sales. So, besides the new media, books are competing with the old media as well—and with their retailers, too. Although Barnes & Noble already had a publishing component, in January 2003 the company purchased Sterling Publishing, and by 2010 its Nook e-reader had the rights to more than two million titles. Small wonder book sales have shown little growth in the past few years.

Book sales are flat not only because of the increase in affordable and available media but also because there is an oversupply of books. Independent publishers are the biggest contributor to this oversupply. Recent advances in technology have made writing and publishing a book within almost anyone's means. While some of these are hobby books, family histories, print-on-demand (POD) books, vanity press books, and the like, many have poor design and writing, with minimal if any editing, and these titles still clog up the market. This makes it even more difficult for readers to find the good books they're looking for and for serious publishers to make any money on their new ventures.

"While the large publishers consolidate and prune lists, new titles from smaller and fledgling publishers are proliferating," writes Shatzkin. "Over the past decade, new title production, as measured by Bowker's issuance of ISBNs, has increased from 102,000 titles in 1992 to more than 140,000 in 2002." By 2011 there were 347,178 new titles (or a total of three million if you count nontraditional titles that come through reprints, public domain, or POD). According to R.R. Bowker, in 1992 there were about 37,300 active publishers in the United States. The number doubled in 2005 to 73,000, and in 2010 Bowker reported 196,066 active publishers. This number does not always include the author/publishers who work through companies such as Lulu, iUniverse, and Create Space.

Yet despite the glut of books, despite the convoluted way that booksellers deal with publishers, despite the decline in the amount of time spent reading, and despite the generally low profit margins realized by most publishers, creative, passionate, and ambitious people continue to be drawn to publishing. Logic isn't driving most of them; a kind of committed lunacy to sharing their ideas—be they service or entertainment oriented—is. Mark Twain, one of our country's most famous self-publishers, said, "Take an idiot man from a lunatic asylum and marry him to an idiot woman, and the fourth generation of this connection should be a good publisher."

A more contemporary view comes from Robert Lasner, editor-in-chief of the independent house Ig Publishing in Brooklyn, New York: "You will be ignored by everyone—reviewers, other publishers, authors, booksellers. Don't become a small press publisher unless you really love the high financial risk or have a money tree growing in your backyard. It might be romantic and rosy to all you literary types out there, but it's the most thankless, backbreaking work with the lowest profit margin imaginable."

Undaunted? Good. Because readers, writers, teachers, professors, agents, big publishers, reviewers, libraries, bookstores, and even the cashiers at Walmart need you. While it might be the huge advances paid to celebrity authors by the big publishers that dominate the headlines and the best-seller lists, this handful of media conglomerates is not what keeps our industry vital. You and the tens of thousands of other small publishers are the strongest gear in this mechanism we call the U.S. publishing industry.

> *... creative, passionate, and ambitious people continue to be drawn to publishing.*

"What underpins entirely the publishing world is smaller presses," said George Gibson, publisher of Walker Books, a midsize independent publisher with a forty-five-year history of bringing books of merit to market. Walker made those comments in an interview with Gayle Feldman of the nonprofit advocacy group the Council of Literary Magazines and Presses (CLMP). "The big publishers are loath to admit it; there are thousands of these presses, most not in New York, most very small. The American public is incredibly demanding in the diversity of books it seeks and the big publishers couldn't possibly fulfill those wishes, so the small presses collectively fuel the industry with their breadth and passion."

You trade in words. Draft your own version of The *Oath of a Freeman*, and live and work according to your own mission. Maybe you will be the publisher of the next Walt Whitman or Beatrix Potter or Sherman Alexie. Or even J. K. Rowling or John Grisham. Look at the new releases from conglomerate publishers and it's obvious that the world of big publishing has very little to do with writing ability, civic responsibility, or new ideas. It's about making money. End of mission. That leaves a lot of latitude for the small, self-, independent, and literary publishers to grow and, yes, prosper. The book trade is hungry for your talent, sense of social duty, and new ideas. And, you'll be paid handsomely for them.

Section I
Product and Price

---

*"The most important advice I would suggest to
beginning writers: try to leave out the parts that readers skip."*
—ELMORE LEONARD

Let's build your book. Working under the assumption that you have a fairly complete manuscript at the ready, this section focuses on the various aspects of book production that will make your book rise above the rest. We'll look at setting a solid foundation for your book through the use of an editor, creating a catchy and powerful title, designing a beautiful interior and exterior (for print and e-books), and, finally, how you should price your final product.

> *"The cat sat on the mat is not a story.*
> *The cat sat on the other cat's mat is a story."*
> —JOHN LE CARRÉ

Ready to Kill Some Trees?

Make Your Book Worth the Wood

When it comes to how-to books about publishing, there's no shortage of general information out there about marketing, publicity, getting your book published by a big publisher, setting up book signings, identifying niche markets, etc. Most of the books available today written specifically about independent publishing are either woefully outdated or dangerously incomplete. Still, if you flip through them, do a day's worth of searches on the Internet, check out some back issues of writing and publishing magazines from the library, and make a few phone calls, the rudimentary information about what it takes to publish a book is out there. As a matter of fact, the dream of publication is more accessible than ever since subsidy publishers started taking advantage of new technologies.

"A best seller in thirty days! Sell thousands of books! Tricks of the trade!" But none of it addresses whether your book is any good.

Now wait just a cherry-picking minute, you're thinking right about now. You're more than happy to take our advice about Baker & Taylor and IndieBound and big-box stores and book clubs, but content and style and expression? That's the one place you know what you're doing, right? Well, indulge us for a couple of pages.

Examine your motivations for writing the book in the first place. Harold Bloom said, "The purpose of reading is to give us the blessing of more life." Do you have a story to tell that simply would not stay in your memory or imagination? Have you created a new way of completing some everyday chore that will make all of our lives easier? Perhaps you've led an interesting and drama-filled life and writing about it is tantamount to therapy. Or maybe your motivations are more practical. Do you possess knowledge and perspective from your choice of career and, by writing a book about it, hope to establish yourself as an expert in your field? Maybe you just want recognition. And money.

Whatever topic your book addresses, whether it's nonfiction, fiction, memoir, or poetry, whatever your reasons for writing and/or publishing it, and whether it's your first book or your fifty-first, the only way to achieve your goal for the book is to make it good.

"What I have said for years and years and years is that a major problem we have in our society is that we don't have many good writers or good artists," wrote independent publisher Alan Canton in one of his "Saturday Rant" columns titled "Don't Publish Crap, Don't Buy Crap" and published on BlogSpot.com. "You can debate the hell out of this, but the bottom line is so much of the stuff that we are presented with is plain old unadulterated crap. These are great times to be a writer or an artist or a musician. And because of it, everyone and their dog thinks they can be one ... and the majority of them are just plain terrible. Thus, we are deluged with crap. The bestseller lists are for the most part crap. The hype is crap. Most of the 'airplane' books are crap. What is promoted by the mass media is crap."

Are you publishing crap?

In August of 1940, as World War II raged, Sir Winston Churchill visited the Fighter Command airfields in southern England. The prime minister later said he was awed by the prowess and devotion of these lone airmen who had the potential to change the outcome of the war simply by their bravery and wits. "Never in the field of human conflict was so much owed by so many to so few," Churchill told the House of Commons in a now famous speech.

In 2012, as the publishing war rages on and readers are besieged by the release of some hundreds of thousands of new books every year, we are awed by the sheer output of small, self-, independent, literary, conglomerate, and especially subsidy publishers. Never in the field of human expression was so much crap published by so many and read by so few.

Who, then, is going to read your book? Or, rather, if a tree falls in the forest and is made into a book, will anybody read it? Though you may think that your small press run for a single title won't kill too many trees, book publishing has a tremendous impact on the environment—another reason not to publish crap.

American book publishers, especially, are relentless consumers of paper. According to the Green Press Initiative, a group that has been working to mitigate the environmental impact of book publishing, printing all of our books accounts for 5 to 7 percent of the worldwide paper market. One million tons of paper, made from more than thirty million trees, are used by U.S. book publishers every year.

Bad for the environment means bad for business means bad for your bottom line. Publishing crap is bad for the environment; you call them tree huggers, and they call you tree killers, but name-calling aside, many people identify themselves as environmentalists, and the most adamant among them even urge their followers either to borrow books from a public library or from friends or to buy used books. Do you think that claim is strongest when someone wants to purchase *The Art of the Commonplace*, a collection of Wendell Berry's essays, or when he or she picks up a copy of *Wired for Chaos, Badass Sci-Fi, More Blood, More Pain*? One is a collection of a treasured writer's thoughts on capitalism, the natural world, urban culture, and morality, while the other is a subsidy-published gratuitously violent mishmash with nearly unreadable interior design.

All right, now say that the environmental issue doesn't apply to you because you're not planning to kill any trees. You're publishing your manuscript straight to an e-book, possibly doing print-on-demand (POD) or only a very small printing run. But you're going to monitor the tree killing very carefully. For this, we commend you. Yes, the advent of the e-book has been hailed as one of the most environmentally friendly technologies of the publishing world, and, yes, it is important to look into the POD market or print on recycled paper and so on. But that doesn't change the basic, bare-bones argument here: even if you're putting out only an e-book, you still can't publish crap.

Take five or ten minutes, the next time you're on Amazon, and type in "ebook." Odds are you will be getting three million–plus results. And of these three million e-books, it seems a bit unlikely that 100 percent (or even 75 percent) are quality books. The first search result I got was *How to Write and Publish Your Own eBook in as Little as 7 Days*, which fits perfectly with the stigma of straight-to-e-book books: they can be written and published in seven days. You do not want to be listed among the ranks of one-week wonders. Oh, no. You want your name said in the same sentence with Tolkien or Stephen King or Suzanne Collins. So even if you're not planning a ten-thousand-book print run, remember that what's inside of your book (or what's in your EPUB file) really matters.

Don't think that since you're a small publisher without the resources of the New York publishing houses quality is beyond your reach. On the contrary, your size is a tremendous advantage. Being small, you have the power of decision making. You can decide when a book is finished, not some hierarchical editorial department.

You can proofread the bluelines one more time, without throwing off the production people. You can choose what information to include in the manuscript, not a dollar-driven marketing department.

Publisher's Row holds no quarter with Rick Russell, proprietor of ABE and publisher of *Bookmen's Weekly*. "Billy O'Kane's review of *Blood Cake Vendor* by J. L. Navarro (iUniverse; 512 Pages; $36.95) and its subsequent discussion got me to thinking (and possibly slicing my throat with this editorial)," Russell writes in *A Bad Year for Readers and Dealers*. "*Blood Cake Vendor* fits wonderfully with the titles below. In fact, of the group it is one of the better ones. Never once, since I began selling books in 1973 have I failed to sock away at least one book by a major publisher that I didn't expect to appreciate, until this year. So, J. L., get your negotiation skills together and get your hardcover price down to $26.95 so you can compete, because *Blood Cake Vendor* has a better shot at becoming a collectible than these godawful insults to human intelligence, otherwise known as the output of major publishers in the United States in the year of our Lord 2004."

The objects of Russell's scorn?

Bobby Fischer Goes to War: How the Soviets Lost the Most Extraordinary Chess Match of All Time by David Edmonds and John Eidinow, published by HarperCollins: "Bobby Fischer lives in Iceland, and this book belongs there, outside." *A Chance Meeting: Intertwined Lives of American Writers and Artists, 1854–1967* by Rachel Cohen, published by Random House: "A collection of 36 hack written press releases." *Hip* by John Leland (Ecco/HarperCollins; 405 pages; $26.95): "A whole book to define 'hip' written by a square."

Finally, Russell slams *The Man Who Outgrew His Prison Cell: Confessions of a Bank Robber* by Joe Loya, published by Harper Collins: "When will major publishers stop publishing ex-cons who can't write well? Convinces me that your shot at publishing a book is probably better as an illiterate robber, stupid enough to get caught, than it is to be someone who actually studied literature."

Sometimes, authors and publishers produce a bad book because they don't know any better. Most, though, would never admit it. "I've put books out there that were crap," responded one writer and publisher. "I knew it was crap, but there was a deadline, and you know that drill. I see a lot of titles that no self-respecting publisher in his/her right mind could say, 'This is good work.' Sure, they sell. But crap sells, as we all know. My thesis is that quality will sell even better if we ever bother to take the time and effort to create it."

Author Ben Marcus is brave enough to admit he's written a bad book that got published. Marcus used what he says he thought of as "miserably bad" writing in his novel *Notable American Women* published by Vintage Books in 2001 as fodder for an essay on the topic published on McSweeny.net, the online component of *McSweeny's Quarterly Concern*, a literary journal. "Maybe I wrote a bad book so that I would have something more concrete to apologize about," wrote Marcus in the essay titled simply "I Wrote a Bad Book." "Just another bad attempt to keep attention, which I do not deserve, focused on me. I cannot sustain that attention, nor will it be rewarded. It seems that even my remorse can manage to be self-serving. You won't hear from me again. If you do, you are entitled to use your hands to stop me. You may use force and feel justified. To see to it that I stop. To smother my little, miserable self. It would be best for all involved."

Marcus could have been being a little hard on himself. A *Library Journal* reviewer called the novel "a difficult read for many" but said it would "surely stand the test of time as a genuinely important book" and recommended it for all collections. *Publishers Weekly* said the work contained "conceptual daring, deadpan humor and dizzying forays into allegory," and an *Esquire Magazine* reviewer said it was a "stunning, strange and beautiful novel."

What is the true test of whether you're investing your time, energy, and the world's trees in a worthy book? In your heart of hearts, you already know the answer. While much of this book is devoted to steering you away from making costly mistakes and giving you ideas to make your publishing venture profitable so that you can publish more (good) books, this section is just meant as a catch-your-shirt-on-a-tree-branch attention getter. Make sure that what you publish has value. You certainly don't want to be the after-the-fact inspiration for comedian Milton Berle's corny one-liner: "He was such a bad writer they revoked his poetic license."

"The difference between the right word and the almost right word is the difference between lightning and lightning bug."

—MARK TWAIN

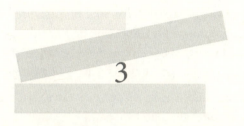

A Great Title

Grab Attention, Sell More Books

The words that comprise the title of your book, though few, are some of the most important ones you'll write on the whole project. If you doubt that, consider this: do you think John Gray would have sold more than eleven million copies of *Men Are from Mars, Women Are from Venus* if he had stuck with his original title for the book, which was *What Your Mother Couldn't Tell You and What Your Father Didn't Know?* Would you have picked it up, carried it to the checkout, and whipped out $16.95 if it had that title?

And would F. Scott Fitzgerald's novel of vacant excess, *The Great Gatsby*, have achieved classic status if its title had remained *The High Bouncing Lover* or *On the Road to West Egg*? Of course, the book would still contain Fitzgerald's impossibly accurate yet youthful descriptions of East Coast wealth and evocative passages such as: "Over the great bridge, with the sunlight through the girders making a constant flicker upon the moving cars, with the city rising up across the river in white heaps and sugar lumps all built with a wish out of non-olfactory money. The city seen from the Queensboro Bridge is always the city seen for the first time, in its first wild promise of all the mystery and the beauty in the world." But would the reader have known that from the title? Possibly not. Fitzgerald's other works also had lackluster working titles: *This Side of Paradise* had been called *The Romantic Egoist and the Education of a Personage*. *The Beautiful and the Damned* was first called *The Flight of the Rocket*. And *Tender Is the Night* was originally shackled with *The Melarky Case*.

Conventional publishing wisdom dictates that a good title can't sell a bad book but that a bad title can keep customers away from a good book. On a recent trip to our local independent bookstore, Horizon Books on Front Street in Traverse City, I scanned the shelves and found the following titles: *The Autobiography of a Yankee Mariner*, *The Grand Idea*, *Morning in America*, *American Colonies*, *God's Children*, *Public Intellectuals*, *Irish Spirituality*, *Visions of Paradise*, *The Northern Forest*, and *Grace and Power*. These titles, while perfectly serviceable, don't make me want to read the books. They sound more like words you'd type into a search engine than book titles.

If a reader has to ask, "What's it about?" you've got the wrong title.

Would you check these books out? Would you buy them at a bookstore? Would you pull them off the shelf and flip through their pages, hoping they'd have something useful or entertaining or absorbing to say? Probably not, right? The titles just don't draw you in. And, as a potential reader, you're bound to think that if the titles are poorly written, the rest of the book might be, too. Surely, you can think of better titles than these. Apply that creativity to your own work. Dig through your notes, or your manuscript, or your imagination for a detail that could develop into a catchy title. Especially for nonfiction, both your title and your subtitle should work as a powerful selling tool, and every single word needs to earn its place in the toolbox.

"Writing a book that lacks a title feels a bit like owning a car with no license plates," writes novelist Nicholas Weinstock in an essay in *Poets & Writers* magazine. "Sturdy and stylish as the vehicle might be, as smoothly as the narrative may be running, the thing will not be allowed in public without some assortment of letters riveted squarely to the front."

If you're stuck and having difficulty making progress on your book because you can't think of the perfect title, choose a working title now and vow to improve upon it as you complete your manuscript. As a general rule, try for a short attention grabber. Use your subtitle to describe the benefits the reader will gain from your book. The job of the subtitle is to let the readers know that they can't live without your book. It's fine and even helpful to use humor, but make sure you avoid clichés, trendy sayings that will be out of fashion by the time your book is printed, and anything your readers would consider "corny" or "cheesy." Make your subtitle catchy, but keep it relevant. According to publishing consultant Judy Collins, your potential readers will spend only four seconds looking at the cover of your book and eight seconds looking at the back cover. The American Booksellers Association puts that figure at 1.5 seconds for the front cover. However tragic, whatever the true number, you don't have long to make a sale.

"You and I know, but most authors don't, how little time a sales rep has to pitch a book to a bookseller," said former Routledge Publishing Director William Germano in a 2001 chat on the website of *The Chronicle of Higher Education*, www.chronicle.com. "The author spends ten years writing it, we spend a year making it, and the poor sales rep has a few seconds."

Author, speaker, and founding president of the Colorado National Speakers Association Joe Sabah has developed five rules to writing effective titles:

1. If the reader has to ask, "What's it about?" you've got the wrong title.

2. The title must meet a perceived need or want of the reader.

3. Even though thousands of authors have used them, the words "How to" are still great first words for a title.

4. Upgrade the obvious. For example, Sabah had given a seminar titled "How to Get the Job You Want." When he changed the title to "How to Get the Job You Really Want and Get Employers to Call You," attendance dramatically increased. His book of the same name has garnered $357,000 in sales and gotten him booked on 628 radio talk shows.

5. Extol benefits, benefits, benefits.

"Here's the formula to help you create your speech title that sizzles and sells," writes Sabah. "First ask six to eight friends over for dinner and a brainstorming session. Yes, you feed them first. Next, without any explanation, read your title to your friends, pause, repeat it a second time. Then ask them to vote (with a show of hands) 'How many of you would give this a 10, 9, 8, 7, etc.' This will give you the pulse of your audience. Ask for feedback. 'Why did you give this an eight?' 'Why did you give this a two?' Remember, people love to give their opinions. Companies pay big money for surveying what people want; they call it market research."

Sabah further suggests asking those same friends for ideas to strengthen your title. Select the best five or ten titles and show them to a dozen additional friends, asking them to vote for their favorite. This process should give you, at the very least, a solid working title.

Collins suggests that writers have a working title before they even begin their first chapter. To get ideas, she says, head out to your local bookstore, go directly to the section where your book would be stocked, and choose the five books that attract you. Take along colored markers and sketch the entire cover, with the title and cover colors intact. Use these sketches to make your book title the best of the bunch.

"Don't be a sissy with your book title," she writes. "People do judge a book by its title. It must be so outstanding and catchy it compels the reader to look further on the back cover. It must be easy to say, easy to remember and clear in meaning."

Fiction writers might want to consider an oxymoronic title. An oxymoron, according to Dr. Mardy Grothe, author of *Oxymoronica: Paradoxical Wit and Wisdom from History's Greatest Wordsmiths*, is "any compilation of phrases or quotations that initially appear illogical or nonsensical, but upon reflection, make a good deal of sense and are often profoundly true." The play on words indicative of an oxymoron should appeal to the creative nature of fiction writers and readers, and using this literary device could give just the emotional pull a fiction and/or literary writer was seeking to establish in his or her title.

"A well-known example in the intellectual domain is the title of a classic 1950 book by the eminent sociologist David Riesman: *The Lonely Crowd*," says Grothe. "Typically, the concept of loneliness is associated with a solitary individual, but when Riesman oxymoronically linked up 'lonely' and 'crowd', he found a compelling—indeed an unforgettable—way of capturing the alienation of modern society." Some other examples of oxymoronic titles, both fiction and nonfiction, cited by Grothe include *Important Nonsense* by Lionel Abel, *A Gentle Madness: Bibliophiles, Bibliomanes, and the Eternal Passion for Books* by Micholas Basbanes, *Too Much Is Not Enough* by Orson Bean, *Little Big Man* by Thomas Berger, *Alone Together* by Elena Bonner, *Professional Amateur* by T.A. Boyd, *Crazy as a Soup Sandwich* by Harlan Ellison, *The Best Awful* by Carrie Fisher, *Lent: The Slow Fast* by Starkey Flythe, *Darkness Visible* by William Golding, *The Perfect Storm* by Sebastian Junger, and *If You Leave Me, Can I Come Too?* by Cynthia Heimel.

There have also been trends toward the success of one-word titles. Using a single, powerful word for a title has always been a dramatic element used by fiction writers, for example, *Disobedience* by Jane Hamilton, *Plainsong* and *Eventide* by Kent Haruf, *Underworld* by Don DeLillo, *Loverboy* by Victoria Redel, and *Vineland* by Thomas Pynchon. During June 2011, for example,

The New York Times fiction best-seller list included *Room* by Emma Donoghue (at no. 12) and *Betrayal* by Fern Michaels (at no. 21). On the IndieBound nonfiction best-seller lists for the same time period, I found *Bossypants* by Tina Fey (no. 4), *Unbroken* by Laura Hillenbrand (no. 5), and *Incognito* by David Eagleman (no. 13). Other popular books with one-word titles include *Seabiscuit* by Laura Hillenbrand (see a theme?), *Downtown* by Pete Hamill, *Triangle* by David Von Drehle, *Bushworld* by Marureen Dowd, *Wink* by Ed Hotaling, and *Speaker* by Denny Hastert.

Just like writing a well-written book, coming up with a great title usually takes time and thought. Though some authors may have the perfect title just "pop" into their heads, most have to work at it. Don't be too hard on yourself if you're having trouble. Even authors with more than one book under their belts sometimes still have trouble coming up with the perfect title. "Writing the darn stories is easier than naming them," says Harlequin romance author Tanya Michaels, in *Love Notes*, a publication of the Romance Writers of America.

Keep in mind, too, that book titles are not subject to copyright protection. You can, however, apply for a trademark for your title if it is to be used in a series. For example, the Magic School Bus children's educational book series or the *For Dummies* or *For Idiots* books are examples of these. Also make sure you check your title against other books already published or soon to be forthcoming. The last thing you want is for your book title to be exactly the same as, or very similar to, that of another book, especially a high-profile one published by a big publisher.

"The worst case is where a small publisher puts out a book with a conflicting title at almost the same time as a large publisher," publishing consultant and author Pete Masterson told the Pub-Forum newsgroup. "Orders almost inevitably go to the large publisher. It's especially difficult if the topic is closely related. A terrible example is a book by one of my clients. His book is resting at 970,000 sales rank at Amazon. Two others from larger publishers are ranked in the 40,000 bracket. When you search for his title, it's listed 13 out of 14 and is a long scroll down the page. Of course, the two other books are at the top of the list. So here the title is crushed by the popularity of the name. The book, however, is actually an excellent study of the primal emotions that drive all of us." Masterson is the author of *Book Design and Production: A Guide for Authors and Publishers* and founder of Aeonix Publishing Group.

Try some of the above suggestions or work out your own system, but don't slight your title. And once you have it, make your great title work for you. Print it on business cards to be distributed at conferences. Put it on a few T-shirts or coffee mugs to give to your friends and fans. Reserve the URL for web marketing, and say it out loud a few times, even if the only ones who first hear it are your cats. You want it to roll naturally off your tongue. Soon, your audience will have two feet, not four, and be interested in what you have to say about your book—the one with the great title—not because you fill their food dish but because you fill their mind.

"Good stories are not written. They are rewritten."
—PHYLLIS WHITNEY

SETTING THE FOUNDATION

Realizing Your Editorial Needs

There is little more annoying than finding typos or errors while you're reading a book. Not only are mistakes distracting but also they make you lose a little faith (or a lot, if the wrong "there"/"their"/"they're" was used) in the writer. It's like having cracks in the foundation of your house; if the writing isn't right, then all the rest of it—the cover, the layout, the marketing—is going to come tumbling down. Without the stamp of a brand-name publisher on your book, it's even more important that your writing is flawless (and we mean that in every sense of the word). Spelling, grammar, and content should be top-notch, and unless you're the U.S. National Grammar champ, it's likely that you're going to want to hire another set of eyes for your manuscript.

"It's critical to hire a professional editor unless you have one in the family," says editor Rebecca Chown. "Even then, if this person can't be objective about your writing, you need to find someone who can. Spell-check is correct maybe three-fifths of the time, and an English degree, while helpful for lots of reasons, merely hints at aptitude rather than guarantees thoroughness and quality. It is always sad to see a neat idea compromised by sloppy writing. By this I mean anything from unintentional redundancies, to using the wrong word, to making elementary grammar and punctuation mistakes, to not going beyond the obvious in the writing. Many people get so carried away with an idea that they forget that writing is unforgiving. Many also forget that anticipating the needs of their audience—an important issue that a professional editor always keeps in mind and addresses as needed—is essential. A good editor does not appropriate an author's text—i.e., make it over in his or her own image—but does add a whole lot of polish to what can be a pretty rough diamond."

"Two heads are better than one" holds true when editing; while you, the author, know exactly what you're trying to say, it's not always clear on the page. This is where an editor comes in. And, no, your editor can't be your mom or your boyfriend or the studious-looking girl across the hall (unless, of course, she happens to be a professional editor). You need a pro, someone who knows the ins and outs of book publishing, someone who is paid to have an eagle eye for split infinitives, double spaces, character development, and proper punctuation. Even more important, you want someone who knows the *Chicago Manual of Style* (CMS) like the back of his or her hand. While there are several different style guides out there (you've probably used MLA or APA at some point in your life), the CMS is the definitive guide for books. It is imperative that your writing conforms to CMS standards, and hiring a professional editor will make sure that's the case.

Generally speaking, there are four different types of editing: genre content editing, content editing, copy/line editing, and proofreading. We'll go through each one and tell you when to use which editor and what results you should be expecting.

Genre Content Editing

What is it?

Service companies or publishers often provide a professional editor who specializes in the field your book discusses. We're talking both an expert on the topic and an excellent writer, someone who knows the material and is well versed in the CMS and the type of writing that your genre demands. This editor will evaluate the manuscript based on the content and point out inconsistencies, areas for revision, organization, redevelopment, and/or content additions and deletions.

When do I use a genre content editor?

You'll want to use a genre content editor under fairly specific circumstances. For example, a busy CEO will turn to a genre content editor because he does not have time to write out all of his thoughts and experience. The editor has enough expertise to fill in the blanks and do research and fact-checking. If you are considering this route, once you have a manuscript put together, you'll take it to a genre content editor with questions in mind. Point out sections that need help and explain your needs.

What does it cost?

Genre content editors are on the expensive end, usually asking $80–$120 an hour. Because these editors are very specialized and provide comprehensive services, they are going to do much more than look for minor errors and will contribute a great deal of work to your manuscript. In most cases, you can ask the editor to estimate the number of hours needed for your book and base your decision on that quote.

Content Editing

What is it?

This type of editing is for manuscripts in need of restructuring, redevelopment, or content addition or deletion. A content editor will make suggestions on reorganization of information, content development and new material, rewriting, artwork placement, front and back matter, and overall clarity of writing.

When do I use a content editor?

If your manuscript seems a bit confused, with big chunks missing or sections that don't quite fit together, you'll want a content editor. Or maybe you've been writing your book over the past several years or you want to convert a series of journals into a book. Think of your book as one of those giant thousand-piece puzzles. If you dump out all the pieces at once, it's impossible for anyone (except a content editor!) to make heads or tails of that mess. A content editor takes the pieces and makes them fit together; he or she will smooth transitions, rewrite bits and pieces, and organize your writing so it has structure and flow. Again, you'll want to get your manuscript to a content editor fairly early in the book production process so you can get that all-important other set of eyeballs on your work.

What does it cost?

Content editors usually charge about $60–$80 per hour for their services. Because most people don't need a genre content editor, this type of editing will often be step one in your editing process. The content editor will give your book a higher-level look, so you will still want to employ a line editor and proofreader later on.

Copy/Line Editing

What is it?

This type of edit is for manuscripts that are structurally sound but need evaluation regarding grammar, usage, flow, clarity of writing, spelling, punctuation, and capitalization. A copy edit may also include editing of chapter heads and front and back matter, including the index.

When do I use a copy/line editor?

Every writer writes in his or her own personal style, and copy editors certainly take this into account. There is leeway provided for your voice and style, but a copy editor will make sure that you are using proper grammar with correct and clear form. You'll use a copy editor right away on your manuscript (if you are using a content editor, this is step two).

How much does it cost?

This type of editing usually ranges from $40 to $60 per hour of work. While copy editors aren't going into the same depth of a content editor, it is likely that they will make some significant changes to your writing and help you meet the CMS guidelines.

Before and After

Here is an example from one of our book clients, Dan Prisciotta's *Defend Your Wealth*.

Initial:

> A second set of objectives dealt with the disposition of the remaining 2/3rds of the deceased brother's estate. Specifically, to keep the business up and running – there were over 200 employees - all of whom depended upon the business flourishing in order to support themselves and their families. In other words, what was the immediate business succession plan now that the Founder was gone? Equally important, how could we possibly "keep the doors open" with the surviving brother having a fairly short life expectancy himself, AND, address the estate taxes that must be paid on both the deceased brother's estate (about $45 mil. - note: all estate taxes are due and payable within 9 months of the date of death and must be paid in cash). The estate tax payment issue becomes even worse when the surviving brother passes away. In other words another $15 mil. will be due when the surviving brother dies!

Edited:

A second set of objectives dealt with the disposition of the remaining two-thirds of the deceased brother's estate—specifically, to keep the business up and running. The company employed more than 200 employees, all of whom depended upon the business flourishing in order to support themselves and their families. In other words, what was the immediate business succession plan now that the founder was gone? Equally important, how could we possibly keep the doors open, with the surviving brother having a fairly short life expectancy himself, and address the estate taxes to be paid upon both the deceased brother's estate (about $45 million—note that all estate taxes are due and payable within nine months of the date of death and must be paid in cash) and the surviving brother's estate? The total estate tax payment issue became even worse when the surviving brother passed away. In other words, another $15 million would be due when the surviving brother died!

Proofreading

What is it?

Proofreading involves a final reading of the text to make sure all edits were made and no new errors were introduced into the manuscript during the editing stages. Oftentimes the proofreader will look for errors in grammar, spelling, punctuation, and capitalization, as well as conformity to the CMS.

When do I use a proofreader?

Since this will be your final cleanup, proofreading generally takes place on a document that has had a bit of work done to it. If you chose to use a content and/or copy editor, proofreading is the last editorial step. Some detailed authors (with a little more money to burn) will do several proofreads, and major editors can spend years on books for the Big Six publishers.

How much does it cost?

This is your cheapest option, as proofreaders generally cost between $20 and $40 per hour. You might be tempted to skip straight to proofreading, since that's what you had a tutor do with your college essays, but be wary. While proofreaders are very good at their jobs, they aren't going to go into the same detail that copy, content, and genre editors do. They will stick to the mechanics and minor errors; it's not their job to find flaw with your main character or point out the glaring contradiction in chapter 22.

Before and After

Below is a brief example of the work a proofreader will do (the book is *Change One Letter, Change Your Future* by W. Patrick Clarke). Look for the small changes that were made, all so that the manuscript would conform to the CMS!

Initial:

If you're thinking of starting your own financial management business—or, by chance, you already have one that's up and running—how would you like that business to look and function? Put another way—in the best of all possible worlds, what would you want your business to look like?

Edited:

If you're thinking of starting your own financial-management business—or you already have one that's up and running—how would you like that business to look and function? Put another way: in the best of all possible worlds, what would you want your business to look like?

FAQ and Further Recommendations

1. *My budget does not allow for four different editors. What is the most cost-effective path?*

    If you don't have the funds for a complete editorial foray, it's best to invest in a copy editor and a proofreader.

These two editors can ferret out the majority of the problems with your book, though you do lose the opportunity for a lot of attention to content.

2. *How do I find an editor?*

    There are many different options out there. Your best bet is to look for an accredited association of editors. They have internal standards, such as a certain number of years in the business, a degree in a certain field, XYZ coursework in college, etc., that make these candidates preapproved for your book. Start by looking around on the Internet, work through a book service company, or ask other publisher and author friends for advice.

3. *How do I know when I find a good editor?*

    Always ask for samples and examples. Good editors will have references and works that they can show you to prove their worth. Also, if your editor is part of an accredited association, he or she is more likely to have the abilities and experience that you desire. Finally, remember that you get what you pay for; if someone offers you editing services at an unreasonably low price, he or she may not turn out high-quality work.

4. *How much change should I expect in my manuscript?*

    This depends on what type of editor you hired. Genre and content editors will make the most perceptible changes, though copy editors and proofreaders can also make lots of changes in structure and grammar, though these are a bit less noticeable in comparison. Before getting started on the project, talk to your editor about how much you want and expect, and stay in touch throughout the process to make sure you are comfortable with the changes. That being said, don't take editors' advice too lightly—they certainly know what they're doing.

What Can I Do on My Own?

"Writers should get their books in the best possible shape they are capable of," Chown says, "and then hire a professional editor and/or proofreader (oftentimes these individuals are one and the same). Depending on the author's experience, comfort level with editing, knowledge of what their book may be lacking, and the like, they can give an editor/proofreader some guidance, but a professional editor will also be able to read a manuscript, identify any weaknesses, and begin to address them."

There are a few steps you can take before getting set up with an editor. Most are simple, and a few you may have never thought of. Keep in mind that the last suggestion is the most important of all.

- **Spell-check:** Sounds obvious but you would be amazed at how few people take advantage of spell-check options in their word-processing programs. Don't blindly hit "change" for every highlighted word or phrase; computers make mistakes, too. Look carefully at every red- or green-underlined word so that you'll avoid similar mistakes in the future.
- **Read it aloud:** What may sound great on the page may not sound as perfect when read out loud. You can catch a lot of phrasing and structural errors this way (and practice your public speaking skills).
- **Read it backward:** This is a good trick of the trade. The more time you've spent with your manuscript, the more likely it is that your brain will fill in words or skip over errors. Reading backward will turn up tons of minor mistakes in spelling, punctuation, and grammar.
- **Have a friend read it:** Eyes, eyes, eyes. You probably don't want to subject your closest friends to a four-hundred-page brick, so give them bits and pieces that you think are both good and bad (that way you can find out whether you're right).

- **Have an acquaintance read it:** This is even more important than having a friend look at your book. If you have someone in your peripheral group of friends or contacts, say, a former college professor, whom you trust and who would be willing to do you a favor, contact him or her immediately. An acquaintance is more likely to be honest with you, where your friends might not be, because an acquaintance is less concerned about your feelings and more concerned about your writing.

Now go get an editor. Once you've done one or two or all of the above suggestions, start hunting for a pro and prepare to be amazed at the help he or she will provide.

> "In a badly designed book, the letters mill and stand like starving horses in a field. In a book designed by rote, they sit like stale bread and mutton on the page. In a well-made book, where designer, compositor and printer have all done their jobs, no matter how many thousands of lines and pages, the letters are alive. They dance in their seats. Sometimes they rise and dance in the margins and aisles."
>
> —ROBERT BRINGHURST

5

Designing Your Book

Pretty Gets Noticed

Because the best design is simple and sensible and instinctual and because virtually everyone knows it when he or she sees it, many small and self-publishers think they can design their own books. This is especially true today, with so many computer programs available that make the job seem easy. Our advice? Don't do it. If you can't afford to hire a designer for your book, you can't afford to publish. Wait until you can. Even in the world of words, where intellect reigns, pretty still gets you noticed—and your book sold. In the meantime, work on other aspects of your publishing program, such as a marketing plan, your pitch to distributors, a sample press release, quotes from printers, etc.

If you're put off by the initial expense, don't be. In the long run, hiring a designer—and this assumes that whomever you hire is talented and experienced—will save you money. First, you won't have to invest in new software programs and expensive computer hardware to run them, and second, you'll sell many more copies of your book if it is designed by a professional than if it is designed by you. That truth might be painful—but not nearly as painful as looking at a garage full of ugly books five years after they've been printed.

"Design informs even the simplest structure, whether of brick and steel or of prose," writes E. B. White in the third edition of the classic *The Elements of Style* (William Strunk Jr. is, of course, the original author, but White updated the book after Strunk died). "Columbus didn't just sail, he sailed west, and the New World took shape from this simple and, we now think, sensible design."

Exterior Design

Have you ever noticed how the entryways of some houses make you feel welcomed, at ease, and relaxed enough to stay a while, whereas the look of others keeps you stuck out on the front stoop? Sometimes, these feelings can come unbidden and have little to do with who opens the door. You might not be exactly sure why you feel the way you do, but you know immediately whether you want to take the next step. Pleasing entryways, even those belonging to strangers, are clean and uncluttered, with a few items of interest strategically placed, leading your eye deeper into the rest of the house. On the other hand, your best friend could open her door to you, but if all you see are stacks of shoes to trip over, a jumble of coats on the floor, and a broken umbrella in the corner, you're apt to ask her to meet you at a coffee shop down the street instead of in her kitchen. Who wants to wade through all that junk just to get to the good stuff?

It's the same with books. Recognizing good design is instinctual; you know it when you see it. We'll touch on a few of the most important design points for the exterior of your book and point you toward helpful websites and books that can give you more details.

Misspelled words and/or profanity in the title, subtitle, or cover copy

The most common misspelled word on the interior of books, in Jenkins Group's experience, anyway, is "foreword." Far too many people, most who should know better, spell it "forward." A misspelled word in the title is even worse. Once it's printed, it stands out as if it were on a marquee, and you wonder how you ever missed it in the proof stage. The only option is to reprint. As far as using profanity in the title or subtitle of your book, despite how far our collective vernacular has plunged in recent years, putting these words on a book cover is still usually perceived as tacky. Even books about swearing have tame-sounding titles, such as *Bawdy Language* by Lawrence Paros or *The Little Book of Essential Foreign Swear Words* by Emma Burgess, and leave out the profanity. The last thing you want to do is offend a potential reader before he or she even cracks the cover.

One recent example that has profited despite its title is Akashic Books' *Go the F**k to Sleep*, often called a children's book for grown-ups. Published in 2011, writer Adam Mansbach and illustrator Ricardo Cortés pushed the boundaries of bedtime stories (though we don't recommend reading this to your little one) and succeeded. Actor Samuel L. Jackson read the story on the David Letterman show and went on to read the audiobook version for Audible.com. It was also listed as a *New York Times* best seller. Keep in mind that *Go the F**k to Sleep* is more of a novelty book and is geared toward sleep-deprived parents at their wits' end. While this particular book is funny and often extremely true, we still suggest cleaning up your title language to appeal to the broadest market of publishers, distributors, and readers.

Your book cover

What do you think of this front cover?

What about this one?

THE INDEPENDENT PUBLISHER

WHAT ARE YOUR THOUGHTS ON THIS ONE?

Communication Land Mines!

18 COMMUNICATION CATASTROPHES AND HOW TO AVOID THEM

Marty Clarke

And this?

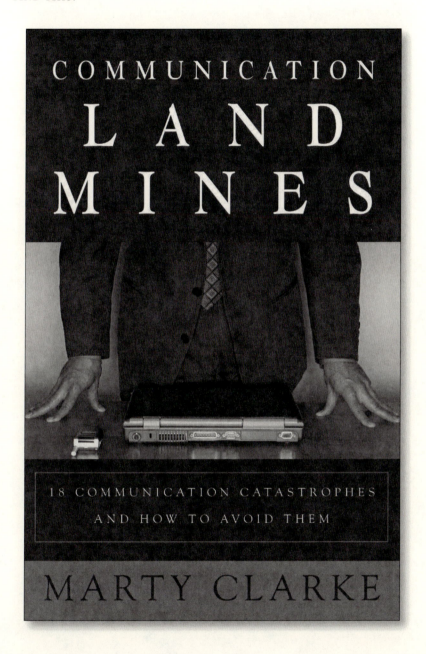

The Independent Publisher

What do you think of this one?

How about this?

The first covers were the author's original design; the second showcased the redesign created at Jenkins Group. A bit of an improvement, don't you think?

Everyone—and I mean everyone—judges a book by its cover. Customers want to see a beautiful, simple, and well-made cover that seems relevant to your title (meaning you shouldn't have a picture of a kid on a bike if your book is about water treatment plants). Here are some dos and don'ts that will help you create the perfect cover.

- Do design your cover so it looks similar to other books in your genre. For example, cookbook covers should probably feature food, and children's books need illustrations.
- Do keep it simple. Busy book covers can distract your reader from your title and often appear cluttered or confused.
- Do use endorsements—sparingly and when they are relevant (and positive). Use one or two short quotes from well-known people or publications.
- Do use appropriate colors. If your book is about ocean travels, use some blues. If it's about the environment, add in some green. The colors you use should complement your title and the theme of your book.
- Don't let your cover image(s) overwhelm your title. Make sure the title is properly positioned on the cover and stands out from the background, unless the topic of your book is invisibility.
- Don't use a small or complicated typeface for the title. Go for a clean and legible typeface for both the title and the subtitle. As a general rule, the size of the title should be considerably larger than that of the subtitle.
- Don't produce a cover that uses cheap materials. Walk around a bookstore or browse your own shelves to find covers that feel and look good and hold up under use.

- Don't expect readers to stick around for a bad cover. As we've told you, you have only a matter of seconds to get your reader interested. So invest, invest, invest in good cover design.

Some great websites to visit for all of your cover questions are www.askthecoverdesigner.com and www.unrulyguides.com. You can find tons of tips and tricks that will guide you to your best cover.

The back of the book

So your front cover got them interested. The true selling point is your back copy (or what's inside the flaps). The copy on a hardcover book flap is fairly straightforward: synopsis, endorsement/blurb, and about the author. Some people like to include excerpts from the book, though this really works well only with sequels.

Figuring out the back of your book can take a little bit more time. Luckily for you, the back copy is created using an easy equation:

BOOK CATEGORY + HEADLINE + COPY (~250 WORDS)
+ TESTIMONIALS/ENDORSEMENTS + AUTHOR BIO AND PHOTO
+ PUBLISHER INFORMATION + PRICE + BARCODE
= BACK OF THE BOOK

If that seems like a lot to remember, don't worry—we aren't going to test you on it. If you turn to the appendix, you'll see that we added the guidelines, for both the front and back cover, that we use here at Jenkins Group. Provide them as a guide to be used by your designer (because you've hired one, right?) and stay involved during your cover production to make sure it's perfect for you and for your readers.

Interior Design

Do you know the difference between serif and sans serif? What kerning is? That different typefaces have different visual sizes? What a descender is? Or x-height? What a word block is? Or a widow or an orphan? All of these elements and many more must be taken into account when designing your interior. Like great athletic prowess, inspired writing, and intricately planned messiness, in the eyes of your reader, the design of the inside of your book should disappear in most places but shine brilliantly where it matters, like chapter title pages, say, or front and end matter.

"[Readers] don't often know a serif from a sans serif," Mayapriya Long of Bookwrights Design posted to the Pub-Forum newsgroup. "They couldn't tell you what about a book made it a breeze to read (not talking about content of text here) or pleasing and well organized. They may not even realize that the book is well-designed, they may just think they are enjoying the read because they feel good that day. The experience is pleasing but they can't tell you why. They don't realize that a well-designed book does that for you."

However, just like you, readers know good design when they see it and are accustomed to books having a certain "look" that, despite the software available, is difficult to duplicate if you are not a trained book designer, wise in the ways of both design principles and the book-printing process. Professional design effortlessly communicates from writer to reader through typefaces, white space, title ornaments, and other devices. Something else Long recommends that publishers consider: books are designed to please not just the reader but also the book industry's "gatekeepers." Reviewers, distributors, sales reps, booksellers, and librarians all will respond well only to a well-designed book.

Having looked through thousands of galleys, review copies, bound manuscripts, and finished books from publishers of every size, designers have developed a list of faux pas that will, if found, immediately mark your book as being produced by an amateur and therefore unworthy of a review (or, subsequently, of a distributor contract, bookstore order, media attention, book award, gold star, cookie, or prize at the bottom of the box). Though long, this list is admittedly incomplete, as new blunders take awkward bounces out of keyboards and subsequently land on, and in, new books every day. Avoid all of these by hiring an experienced, competent book designer.

Typographical errors

The most common one of these is something you would never catch unless you're a professional typesetter or designer. Most writers were taught to type by high-school typing teachers or by business-school teachers who demanded two spaces after every period, question mark, colon, or semicolon. Ruler to the fingers or, at the very least, a paper assaulted with red pen marks if you didn't comply. Printed books, however, should have only a single space after such punctuation marks. This is because letters on a typewriter or, today, those generated from a computer keyboard have a fixed size, whereas letters that are typeset have a proportional size. If you're guilty of using two spaces after every end-of-sentence punctuation mark, your designer may ask you to use the "search and replace" function in your electronic document before submitting it. Other designers will do this task for you. And skip the automatic tab key, as well. It adds way too much space and makes justifying paragraphs difficult.

Another typographical error that, if used, will mark your book as being one produced by an amateur is the use of underlined words. Substitute italics or bold print instead. Let underlining die a good death on your mildewed college research papers stuck in a drawer somewhere. Underlining slows a reader down and can interfere with some letters.

Now, just because we suggested using those two tactics when you need to emphasize something does not give you permission to spread around italics and bold like an abstract painter spreads paint. Use them sparingly. Those three words bear repeating. Use them sparingly. We've seen many poorly produced books with entire paragraphs and sometimes even whole chapters of italicized or bold text. This does not make your point with your readers unless your point is to irritate, tire, and repulse them. Reading big chunks of this kind of printing feels like being yelled at. And, while a little yelling might be effective, a lot of it just makes readers turn—or run—away.

Low-Quality Paper and Printing

Put your researching cap on. Unless you are working through a tried-and-true publisher (and sometimes even then), you're going to have to know your way around paper and printing. If a vendor offers you a radically cheap price, you could end up having your book printed on tissue paper. If you choose to get printing quotes yourself, be sure you are educated in the details and terminology. Ask the printer for paper samples and examples of books the company has done so you can see the words, the saturation of the ink, and how images look on that particular stock.

When it comes to getting a printer, look for previous work and recommendations. Again, stay on top of the technology and capabilities of a printer, such as whether it uses offset or digital printing. Hunt around before making your choice and always, always ask for samples.

Faulty Pagination

Page numbers, called folios by designers, are useful and sought after by your reader in any document longer than two pages. Though most are placed on the bottom outside corner of the page, they can be just as pleasing at the top outside corner or centered on the bottom of the page. Keep in mind that if your book is one apt to be flipped through, page numbers at the bottom corner will be the most useful to your reader. Brightly colored page numbers or a font radically different from the one used in the body of the text is to be avoided except in the cases of art books or some gift books. The goal of a page number is to be easily seen when the reader is specifically looking for it but to disappear at all other times.

Narrow Margins

What your book has to say is so important that you've got to pack as much on every page as possible, right? Well, hold on. If it's really that important—and if it's not, why are you publishing it?—then your reader is going to be willing to turn pages. Amateurs try to save money on printing costs by making the page margins narrower than standard size, thereby printing fewer pages. Bad, bad idea. First off, a bigger book translates as a better value to readers. Second, those narrow margins are exhausting to the eyes. According to Pete Masterson of Aeonix Publishing Group, "The eye needs the 'relief' of unprinted areas to make reading and comprehension easier."

Although there is no exact margin measurement that applies to all books, Yvonne Roehler, creative director, Jenkins Group, notes, "When designing the interior text pages of a text-heavy book with a trim size of 6 × 9, a good rule of thumb is to format the bottom page margin to be the largest, with slightly smaller top and outside margins. My personal preference is to tweak the inside (gutter) margin to be a bit bigger than the outside page margin to ensure my text will not 'fall into the gutter' and be difficult to read. I suggest the gutter margin be a minimum of .625 inches and the outside margin be sized between .7667 and .835. A top margin of .835 paired with a bottom margin of one inch creates a pleasing text design. Books with larger trim sizes can use proportionally larger margins."

Typefaces

As a reader, when you finish a truly satisfying book, what do you do? Turn to the last page just to make sure there isn't anything you missed, right? And what you find, if the book has been crafted as lovingly as it was written, are the words: "A note about the type." There is more to letters than Times New Roman, Helvetica, and Arial, and book designers and typesetters know it. According to *The Elements of Typographic Style*, "Letterforms have tone, timbre, character, just as words and sentences do. The moment a text and a typeface are chosen, two streams of thought, two rhythmical systems, two sets of habits, or if you like, two personalities, intersect. Typography is the art and craft of handling these doubly meaningful bits of information. A good typographer handles them in intelligent, coherent, sensitive ways. When the type is poorly chosen, what the words say linguistically and what the letters imply visually are disharmonious, dishonest, out of tune."

For example, a long endnote in the hardcover first edition of Noel Perrin's *Third Person Rural* published by David R. Godine Publishers reads, in part, "*Third Person Rural* has been set by Dix Type Inc., Syracuse, New York, in Janson, an old style face first issued by Anton Janson in Leipzig between 1660 and 1687, and typical of the Low Country designs broadly disseminated throughout Europe and the British Isles during the seventeenth century. The contemporary versions of this eminently readable and widely employed typeface are based upon type cast from the original matrices, in the possession of the Stempel Type Foundry in Frankfurt, Germany." It stands to reason that a book in which the typeface was chosen so carefully is a book in which equal care was placed in other areas: research, expression, editing, etc.

Too Much Gingerbread

Does your city have a historical neighborhood? If so, there is probably a street or two dominated by Victorian-era homes painted in pastel tones and adorned with wooden curlicues around every porch column, doorframe, roofline, and soffit. The most attractive of these use such ornate decoration for emphasis of the home's best features but still use plain trim in other areas. The tacky ones are loaded down with the stuff, hiding the house's natural lines and making them look like an oversized knickknack. Inside, it's easy to picture the neighborhood crazy lady, babbling nonsense to herself and crocheting lacy hats for her menagerie of cats. The same is true in the use of page decorations, or dingbats, in book design. A little goes a long way, and to overdo it makes you look disorganized at best and at worst maybe even nuts. This is an area in which your designer can really show his or her stuff.

For example, when Mary Sue Englund designed *Keepsakes & Other Stories*, by Jon Hassler, for publisher Afton Historical Society Press, she added a gold line at the top of every page, placing it underneath the author's name on the left-hand pages and the abbreviated title, "Keepsakes," on the right-hand pages. The book is a collection of short stories, and on the opening page of each story, Englund placed a small gold and black woodcut depicting some item relating to the story, framed inside a plain gold square. The element is effective because the gold color is reminiscent of a keepsake, and the use of both the line and the woodcuts is repetitive but sparing.

In a subtler but no less effective use of design, Sarah Olson, working for Academy Chicago Publishers, used a separate font for the first capital letter of each chapter in the novel by Vincent Panella, *Cutter's Island*. This is a common design tactic, though Olson made it quite successful by selecting a font that looked like one that could have been used on a pirate's ransom note or treasure map. The novel is a fictionalized imagining of Caesar during his forty days in captivity after being nabbed by pirates when he was sailing to the Isle of Rhodes.

> *... readers know good design when they see it and are accustomed to books having a certain "look" ...*

Another subtle example can be found in Charles Frazier's National Book Award–winning novel, *Cold Mountain*. For aesthetic or perhaps more personal reasons, Frazier used no quotation marks in his 450-page novel of the Civil War, even though the main character, Inman, has many pointed conversations with people he meets on his long journey from a North Carolina hospital to his home on the mountain of the book's title. Instead, the designer inserted a simple dash at the beginning of each quote—a straightforward solution that quickly disappears in the reader's eye and must have satisfied the author's particularities.

It might be worth noting here that of the examples above, all three were published by independent publishers. Big does not necessarily mean beautiful.

A Cliché on Page 51

This is a bit tongue-in-cheek, but it illustrates a point. When the editor of an independent review journal perused some six hundred books a month in an effort to select just forty for review, this sometimes was one of the eliminating factors she used in her selection process. If two titles had made the initial cut and each appeared relevant and well produced, had an interesting and/or well-regarded author, and had been submitted on time, with good supporting materials, it was always difficult to choose between them. She'd turn to page 51—far enough into the book so that the author should've been in full swing—and look for a cliché. If one title had a glaring one and the other didn't, the latter was sent to a reviewer. The point this illustrates is that your book has to meet high standards in every aspect of its production, from the writing to the editing to the design, because it will all be judged, sooner or later, by someone.

E-Book Design

Although a lot of sites will claim that they can produce your perfect e-book, you can't always trust them. Until computer systems can handle complex figures, tables, photos, sidebars, and other add-ons, you're going to want a computer and a person to help create your e-book, which means you're going to need a pro (picked up on that motif yet?). Check out chapter 6 for the details on e-book conversion and design.

Finding a Designer

OK, OK, you're convinced that you need to hire a professional book designer. How do you find one? What does one charge? And, once you've found someone you may want to hire, how do you know that he or she is the right person to work on your book project?

"My advice for the way to pick a good designer is to look at their work," said Mayapriya Long, of Bookwrights Design. "Look at their client list. If they have a variety of clients from small to larger, if they have done more than one book for their clients who have more than one, if you like their work, if they are respected in the industry, if they are busy—better yet, too busy—then they are probably worthy of the respect they have earned and a good hire. Just as you would not print your book at Joe's commercial printing house, you would print it at a printer who specializes in books, has good work to show, and maybe costs you more. Invest in the look of your book. If it doesn't satisfy both of the audiences above, no one will ever know how good the text is."

By nature, many small publishers are mavericks. They either came up with original ideas for books that didn't fit with any larger publishers or had the ability to recognize those ideas from other writers. As a small publisher, your natural instinct may be to buck the system. And why not? That way of thinking has worked for you in the past, right? Eschewing the status quo may have been the reason you received a book review, or were able to schedule an appointment with a key buyer, or kept your terms in an important author contract. For most books, though, design decisions are not the place to assert your offbeat style. Readers and the book industry will look at a book outside standard perimeters with skepticism and scorn and not with awe for your creative genius. Ignore this advice at your peril.

Registrations and the Copyright Page

Before we wrap up the book design discussion, I would be remiss if I did not mention that the six key industry registrations and the copyright page need to be done the right way. By this, I mean go through the necessary agencies to get your registrations done correctly and make sure your copyright page looks like you know what you are doing. Nothing says "amateur" more to an industry professional (e.g., bookstore buyer, librarian, reviewer) faster than an incomplete or incorrectly laid out copyright page.

You will want to get the following registrations and filings done right:

- International Standard Book Number (ISBN) from R.R. Bowker
- Library of Congress card catalog number (LCCN)
- Cataloging in Publication data

- EAN Bar Code
- Advanced Book Information
- Copyright

If you are in doubt, crack open a recent release from a major royalty publisher and follow that as an example. After all, this is your competition. If your copyright page does not resemble theirs, then you have some work to do.

E-Book Creation and Conversion

A Companion Format to Physical Books

For some of us, e-book conversion is a no-brainer, or even step one in the publishing process. The ease with which you can create an e-book is almost frightening; there are hundreds of websites that offer conversion services, and it is often a far cheaper alternative to a print run. However, "cheap" should never be "free." It's still important to put your best foot forward with your e-book, and a foot is bound to have a price tag of some sort.

For others, e-books are the bane of publishing, degrading the written word and making our beloved physical books obsolete. We've all been there, but if you stick with that mind-set, you will become obsolete. Ignoring e-books is akin to being the crotchety grandmother who refuses to use the Internet or the guy who never bought a DVD player (and certainly won't invest in Blu-ray). E-books are here to stay, and your best bet is to view the e-book as a companion format to print. It is another format that many book buyers are expecting to see, particularly from more sophisticated publishers.

The e-book market now represents about 20 percent of book sales (and rapidly growing) and is a good second income stream for publishers and authors. According to BookStats, in 2011 e-books had a total revenue of $2 billion. Not too shabby for the new kid on the block.

With every passing year, e-book sales are growing dramatically, which is illustrated by the point that anyone writing or publishing today can remember the pre-e-book era. People are reading everywhere and on everything. Portable reading devices have become commonplace, and it's time to move on this trend with a trusted partner. No matter your moral perspective on the e-book revolution, there are some rules of thumb that you should follow when creating your e-book.

E-Book Only

Choosing to publish your book straight to the web is a perfectly viable option. More and more writers are skipping the middleman (print books) and putting their e-books up on Amazon, the iBookstore, or Barnes & Noble.

This method is certainly cost effective; authors rarely pay more than $500 to create an e-book (versus the thousands of dollars that can go into a print run). If you are active on social media and involved in other marketing outlets, you can start generating enough sales to break even and then turn a profit quite quickly.

Take, for example, Amanda Hocking. She began publishing her paranormal romances solely in e-book format in 2010 and managed to sell thousands and thousands of books in the following months. Less than a year after her first book went up on Amazon, she got a contract with St. Martin's Press. Hocking started making money right off the bat (and the $2 million St. Martin's Press deal didn't hurt, either), but she was both writing in a popular genre and using social media to her advantage. She blogged, Facebooked, and tweeted about her books to get awareness and published almost twenty books, all helping to get her name to the top of the Amazon lists.

If you do choose to go to an e-book and bypass a printed book, it is even more important that your book is better than the average. Presentation and design are noticeable when using an e-reader, and as an independent publisher, you'll want your book to rise above the rest.

Choosing a Conversion Service

Whether you're going straight to an e-book or converting your print book, choosing the right conversion service company is key. If you hark back to our previous two chapters, you'll remember that we drove home a point about using a professional for your editorial and interior design needs. This holds true with creating an e-book. You'll want to shy away from the websites that offer you a "cut-and-paste" conversion or promise to have your book ready in ten minutes or less. This is not going to produce the best-looking or best-reading book (if it works at all), and you want the best. We're not saying you should go out and drop a full year's salary on the most elaborate and costly conversion service that you can find, but with e-book conversion, quality, not cost, should be the deciding factor. And, as always, ask for examples of previous work from companies you're considering.

It's also important to find a high-quality conversion process that uses both software *and* humans. Unlike computer-generated scripts, working with real people makes it possible to properly deal with elements such as tables and nonstandard characters and correctly convert them into e-book format. You'll want to find someone who can accurately convert the most complex layout elements to the appropriate XML tags. This includes tables, footnotes, illustrations, chapters, sections, and special characters. In some cases, a typical program can utterly ruin a text that has complex tables or figures, and you'll want a set of human eyes making sure your book isn't published with mistakes.

Unless you're looking to hit only a certain e-book market (e.g., you love Kindle so much that you wouldn't even dream of using EPUB), you will want a conversion service that offers all of the common digital publishing formats for the major e-book standards. Many companies can also start with physical books and do the scanning if you don't have the proper digital form available.

What Format Should You Use?

There are a lot of options when it comes to choosing your e-book format, but we've highlighted the most popular and versatile choices.

- **EPUB:** EPUB is the format for Apple products and Barnes & Noble's Nook and nearly all other e-readers (including smartphones, computers, and tablets). By 2011 it became the most widely supported vendor-independent XML e-book format. EPUB does not run on a Kindle.

- **Amazon Kindle:** This is Amazon's format for Kindle books (and is obviously supported on Kindles). Android and Apple devices can also use this format with the help of apps.

- **KF8:** Kindle Format 8 (KF8) powers the book reader on Kindle Fire. KF8 replaces the Mobi format and adds over 150 new formatting capabilities including support for HTML5 and CSS3. This includes embedded fonts, drop caps, and CSS selectors such as line spacing, alignment, justification, margin, color, style, and border. KF8 also enables fixed layout books.

- **PDF:** PDFs can be read on almost any computer and are everywhere on the Internet. They also work on the Nook, Kindle, and most Apple products.

- **Plain Text:** Almost all e-readers can support plain text, though it certainly has limitations depending on the type of book you're publishing (you can't have much in the way of tables, graphs, photos, or design).

- **HTML:** An HTML e-book requires the Internet and a browser to be downloaded and read.

- **MobiPocket:** This is an XHTML format that is quite similar to the Kindle format. It can be read on Kindles, Apple and Android devices, and most other e-readers and computer platforms.
- **Fixed Layout:** This format is great for coffee-table books, cookbooks, children's books, graphic novels, or anything that you want to have that turn-the-page feel. It is a special EPUB or KF8 version and at the moment can be used only on Apple technology and Kindle Fire.

With all of these choices, which do you choose? We suggest going with EPUB and Kindle; this covers the majority of e-readers and will reach the widest audience. Since technology is changing every other day, sticking with these two basic and popular formats will guarantee that your book will get to your readers. You will need an ISBN for each format you choose, so keep that in mind, too (go to www.bowker.com for more information on obtaining an ISBN).

Once the files are converted, you or your conversion company can upload them to the Amazon store, Apple's iBookstore, and Barnes & Noble, among others. Do this immediately; you don't want to wait a month or two and find that your format has become outdated or obsolete.

Different Types of E-Books

If you've spent any time around an e-reader, you've probably seen the wide range of e-book styles available. Some are black-and-white text, others have photos, and the most complex have interactive links or activities for the reader.

E-books are typically categorized into simple, moderate, and complex in terms of conversion and the book itself. Novels are a good example of simple e-books; they are, for the most part, text only and don't require any fancy figures. A moderate e-book could be a nonfiction piece (such as a history or a biography) that includes some photos or tables. Complex e-books are often figure-heavy business books, cookbooks, or books that have interactive features or links. These books are priced according to their complexity (and thus the amount of time and effort needed to convert them).

How Much Does It Cost?

The cost to convert a book typically ranges between $150 and $500. Aside from complexity, page count can also be a factor in cost. Children's books, due to their brevity, are often one of the cheaper conversion options. In most situations, you want to choose a conversion service that yields both an Amazon Kindle version and an EPUB version, so be sure to mention that when getting your quote.

If the thought of paying $300 for an e-book conversion makes you squirm a little bit, think of it this way: if you do it yourself, you might mess it up. Conversion providers often get clients that spent hours and hours getting their book into e-book format, only to realize they had skipped a step and the book was rejected by the retailers. Or, on the other hand, the author went with a super cheap service and the book came out all wrong. If you drop $300 for a nice-looking e-book, you need to sell only thirty books at $9.99 to make up for that cost (OK, maybe fifty books based on royalty rates). You can sell fifty books, can't you? Of course you can. Especially if your e-book looks professional.

While We're on the Subject ... A Word about Audiobooks

Audiobooks are another alternative to print, but these also need to be done well and marketed appropriately. Audiobook consumers aren't as widespread as print or digital readers, and turning your book into a CD or audio file is a bit costly.

Your budget should include studio time, editing, voice talent, and distribution. A general estimate for these needs: around $3,000. Some books lend themselves to being read aloud (think Harry Potter) where others do not (e.g., books that rely on photos, tables, graphs, and figures). If an audiobook is in your budget and your book will command a market, by all means, record away.

> *"Almost anyone can be an author; the business is to collect money and fame from this state of being."*
>
> —A. A. MILNE

Priced to Sell

What Should I Charge?

Ah, the chapter you've been waiting for. How much can you charge your readers, and how in the world are you going to make a profit? In the past few chapters, you've probably picked up on the importance of putting the time, effort, and professional help into your book. Although you might have more work ahead of you than you had expected, it's going to pay off (regardless of uncertainties in the book market).

The same theory applies to a house. If you hire a good team, build a solid and beautiful house, and keep it in good condition, it's going to sell well on any market at any time.

Print Books

Your first step, both with a print book and an e-book, is to do some research, or what publishers call comparative analysis. Comparative analysis is a comparison between what's out there and what you have to offer. Go to a large bookstore and/or Amazon.com and hunt for books that seem similar to yours. Write down about ten or fifteen popular titles and their new and used prices. This should give you a pretty good idea of the range in prices and what consumers are willing to pay for your genre.

While similar books should have a similar price tag, if your book is unique or better in some way, you can increase the price. For example, say the guy who made billions upon billions with stock options is writing a book. He is the world's leading authority on stocks and is going to divulge his greatest secrets. This is genuinely new and valuable information that consumers can't get anywhere else—and they'll pay top dollar for it. However, these books are few and far between, so unless your book is both radically different *and* exceptionally necessary, stick with the more basic pricing guidelines.

Some books always seem to command a premium, such as hardcover business books published by McGraw-Hill or student textbooks (which you certainly remember all too well). Cookbooks are across the board depending on their binding, images, size, etc. As we mentioned in the first chapter, the Workman *What to Expect* series has done exceptionally well for decades. Not only are these books incredibly comprehensive and well written but also they are priced very competitively.

If your book falls outside these general categories, don't fear. The now popular Klutz Books was once a small press before it was purchased by Scholastic. Klutz made its mark by developing ways to entice customers with extras and unique book packages. Its first book, *Juggling for the Complete Klutz*, provided a set of three juggling balls in addition to the creative how-to manual. Klutz now has books for almost every imaginable activity, including art, jewelry making, paper airplane creation, and more. If your book is a little bit different, think of a clever way to pair it with another product or market it to a certain group. You can get creative with pricing in this situation, but keep your price tag competitive for your market.

Once you've come up with a price range for your book, your next step is to take a look at your budget. While it may not actually happen, the goal is to at least break even. We recommend the optimal 6 : 1 ratio, meaning that if you multiply your production costs by six, you'll get your retail price. You can't always achieve this ratio depending on how many books you print; the larger the print run, the lower your costs, though this isn't always wise for a small publisher. If your price point is high, be sure to market your book even more (never fear, we have plenty of marketing tips in later chapters).

We haven't addressed your first print run much, mostly because it varies greatly from person to person and from publisher to publisher. Our rule of thumb? Print as many books as you think you could sell in twelve to eighteen months. For many authors, this is somewhere between two thousand and five thousand copies. If you're printing (and selling) more or less, your price point can vary quite a bit.

E-Books

Since we've been in the e-book revolution only a short time, there isn't a great deal of information about consumer buying habits. There have been some studies, and some guesses, that generally place the typical e-book price around $9.99 (this estimate is also based on companies such as Amazon that have particular control over pricing). The market is trying to find itself; both publishers and readers know that there are much lower costs involved in e-book production, so almost any sale equals a profit. And there are writers who can sell their books for 99 cents and create a huge social media following, regardless of the quality of the writing.

Oftentimes, authors will use an equation involving their hardcover or paperback book (e.g., paperback price − x% = e-book price). But what is x? Whether you are using a retailer or your own site (or both), pricing your e-book can be tricky. While big houses can pay fifteen employees to research the market, track sales data, and find the magic selling number for their e-book, independent publishers and authors rarely have the labor force to invest in such an endeavor.

"One of the interesting opportunities afforded by e-books is the possibility of flexible pricing," Chad Post of Open Letter Books publishing said. "Right now, we print 3,000 copies of a paperback with a price stamped on it. For all intents and purposes, that's the price until all those copies are sold. Which, as most B-school pricing professors would tell you, is pretty ridiculous. In the e-book world, it's completely possible to discount titles to generate interest, or when an author is appearing on a radio show, etc. One of our ideas is to price the e-book at $7.99 for the month prior to its print release. This would be a way of creating a bit of buzz, and providing a bit of an incentive to buy the book in advance."

Post and Open Letter also decided to try a new tactic with the launch of its e-books. In June 2011, the publisher sold all of its e-books for $4.99. "It was primarily a promotional launch price," Post said. "If we were to put these books out there at $9.99 (which will be the price come July 1st), we wouldn't have gotten nearly as much attention for these books as we did."

Adam Salomone of the Harvard Common Press is on board with Open Letter's adaptable pricing. "I would certainly recommend experimentation," he says. "One thing I think remains true to this day: it's easier to lower prices than raise them. If you have the ability to do so, try to set your prices at a healthy margin, just as a way to test the market and then price downward if needed. This may be difficult for some because of the traditional retail model, where many of those outlets that sell our books either dictate the price at which we sell or don't let publishers change those prices over time. But if you have an outlet through which to do it, you should."

Different Rules for Different E-Books

Of course, there are a variety of different types of e-books that call for changes in pricing. When you create your e-book, you have to choose between what Salomone calls "vanilla e-books"—the bare-bones basic format—and an enhanced book that may have interactive links, photos, etc.

"The vanilla e-book is really just the complete text reproduction with any photos, tables, charts, etc., that one might find in the printed book," Salomone explained. "For the most part, we would price these in conjunction with industry standards, which might be $9.99–$12.99, or in some cases a bit less depending on the subject and size of the book. There is usually enough historical data out there, even in the past 2–3 years, of the growth of the e-book market to justify a specific price for the vanilla e-book as publishers continue to sell into that market.

"With an enhanced e-book, the pricing becomes complicated because of a variety of factors. One would assume that the price should be greater than the vanilla e-book because of all the extra functionality (which could include video, audio, links to resources, slideshows, social sharing features, etc.). But we also have to think comparatively about the pricing issue. If you have a $9.99 vanilla e-book, a $12.99 enhanced e-book, a $24.99 printed hardcopy, and a $2.99 app, all for the same book, is the consumer going to understand what they are getting at each price point? I would say they likely won't. The biggest thing to keep in mind is that pricing cannot happen in a vacuum, and what you charge for each edition may well depend on what you're charging for other editions that are already out there."

Discount Pricing: Proceed with Caution

Now say you're ready to lower the price of your book, whether for a promotion or a sale or just to see whether you can create more interest. If you're selling your e-book on Amazon, pricing between $2.99 and $9.99 will earn you a 70 percent royalty rate, but if you're selling for more or less, your earnings won't be quite as high, only about 35 percent. As a result, this low-price model will not work in the long run. "I can't help but think back to an anecdote that a publishing colleague told to me not too long ago," Salomone said.

"The idea of publisher returns, which in many ways has hobbled our industry indefinitely, was started as a way for one publisher to sell more books to retailers. It was a simple solution then, just as pricing our e-books at 99 cents is now, but eventually it becomes an impossible reality to change. We're at a tipping point and pricing is a huge issue, but we have to be careful to not set our future in stone at a price point that's unsustainable."

It's not just Amazon that is creating this lower price trend; it's the consumers. "I suspect that reader demand will have a huge impact on the e-book price fallout," Post predicts. "It's already become clear that there is a group of readers who spend the majority of their book-buying money on 99-cent e-books. Sure, Amazon allows for the 99-cent e-book to exist, but this is a cultural situation. And as with any other media, when there's a near infinite amount of material—and 3 million plus books published in one year is basically infinite in my mind—the price will fall to zero."

Does Price Indicate Quality?

Another hot-button topic when it comes to e-book pricing is the correlation between price and quality. A sloppy, unedited manuscript can be sold at a dollar alongside a *New York Times* best seller for the same price. How do you price competitively to stay distinct from lower-quality works, and how do you give consumers confidence in your products?

"It's not exactly that price equals quality," Post explained. "I'm sure some cheaper books are incredibly entertaining and generate very loyal fans. My concern is that this huge group of readers is starting to evaluate books on the basis of affordability and not on writing quality. This makes me sound like a dinosaur or an elitist, but I think it's important for culture and society for people to cultivate a sense of taste. By trying to capitalize on price points and the way best-seller lists work, it seems to me that this devalues literature and emphasizes the idea of books as simply a commodity."

Salomone also finds fault in using price to gauge quality. "Unfortunately, while price and quality should correlate, I don't know that they do in all cases," he admitted. "Especially where mainstream publishers are pricing into pretty uniform models in the $9.99–$12.99 price range, it's hard to use that to judge what content to buy. And, when you take into account the growing self-publishing market, where authors are putting out content at a variety of price points, it makes it even more difficult to draw a line in the sand and say, 'At 99 cents or less, you shouldn't buy this.' So while pricing should correlate to quality, I feel there are too many players out there using different price points to say whether or not it truly is a marker for quality."

John Oakes of OR Books takes a different look at the price vs. quality debate. "This is where the worth of a publisher is proven," he said. According to Oakes, publishers need not worry that all authors are going to choose to self-publish instead of working with an established press. "A publisher may be offering a $5 e-book, but because you know what kinds of books he has published, you will know that this work is quality. Now is where you have to trust the name. This relationship makes publishers highly relevant in today's world, and we won't be superannuated unless we refuse to change."

The Bottom Line

As we all know so well, ignoring e-books isn't going to make them go away. Embracing the digital world (and all of its faults) sooner rather than later is the best plan of action. "E-books are integral to what we're all about," Oakes said of OR Books. "We start with the premise that our job as publisher is to present readers with what is called 'platform agnostic' format. Readers ought to be able to get their book in any format that is commonly available, whether it is paperback, HTML, EPUB, or something different. We don't regard the e-book as something tacked on."

In this industry and the e-book market in particular, creativity is key. "What's great about this new world of electronic publishing is that you can be as flexible as you want to be," Oakes said. "Although it's always a matter of opinion when it comes to pricing, I want to encourage consumers to buy the e-book, so I price e-books well under my printed copy." Oakes's strategy is simple and successful and certainly allows for changes and tweaks. Finding the perfect price for your e-book may still require a bit of trial and error, but as an independent publisher, you have the freedom to charge what you feel is right (without worry about shareholders or hundreds of employee payrolls). Start off with what seems to be a competitive price based on your comparative analysis and go from there.

Section II
Place

"Put it before them briefly so they will read it, clearly so they will appreciate it, picturesquely so they will remember it, and above all, accurately so they will be guided by its light."

—JOSEPH PULITZER

The age-old adage "Location, location, location" applies to houses, businesses, and, above all, books. Just as you want the perfect neighborhood in which to raise your kids and own the sweet-spot shop downtown, you want to sell your books in the right stores and on the right websites. This section will cover bookstores (both indie and chain), using Amazon.com and other websites—including your own—to sell your book, the pros and cons of print-on-demand, and how to utilize IndieBound, as well as the importance of getting in on the mass market.

Bookstores

Are They Really the Worst Place to Sell Books?

Author, publisher, consultant, and one of the fathers of the self-publishing movement Dan Poynter originally coined the phrase "The worst place you can try to sell a nonfiction book is in a bookstore." He was talking about revenue, pure and simple, and though he first said it more than thirty years ago, unfortunately (while containing bit of exaggeration), it is essentially still true today.

"I coined that phrase in the mid-1970s," Poynter said. "'Bookstores are a lousy place to sell books.' That is the original quotation, which some people have altered. It is even more true today. Stores concentrate on the best sellers by celebrities who bring an audience with them. Yet, readers of nonfiction want targeted information."

Of course, there are obviously worse places to sell books than in a bookstore. On a card table at the end of your driveway, for example. Or inside a video game arcade. Or on a rocky hillside in the middle of a mountain bike race. But no one would try to sell books in those places. Bookstores, on the other hand, should be a no-brainer, right? You've published a good book with great design that you want to sell; bookstores sell books.

"I love bookstores," writes author/publisher Florrie Binford Kichler in the April 2006 issue of the Publishers Marketing Association's (PMA) newsletter. "I shop in bookstores. I'm in a bookstore every week without fail. Spending money in bookstores is easy. Making money with bookstores is the challenge."

If you publish books, making money selling in bookstores may sound logical, but the book industry is anything but. Consider these (rather horrifying) statistics:

- 35 percent of people in the United States have never been inside a bookstore. — U.S. Census
- Nearly 70 percent of U.S. adults have not been in a bookstore in the past five years. — Library and Information Science News blog
- Bookstore return rates from 1995 to 2010 hover around 37 percent, according to industry sources, including the Association of American Publishers, *Booktech Magazine*, and *Publishers Weekly*.
- Book-retailing superstores such as Barnes & Noble regularly return more than 30 percent of the stock they order. — *The Wall Street Journal*
- 57 percent of new books are not read to completion. — Book Industry Study Group
- 70 percent of the books published do not make a profit. — Book Industry Study Group

"A return rate of 15 percent is considered very good," writes Tom Woll in his book *Publishing for Profit*. "Books are displayed in bookstores for one selling season of four months. Those books that do not sell are returned for a refund. Yes, books may be 'gone today, here tomorrow.'"

Most bookstores, if they even stock your title at all, will want a minimum 40 to 55 percent discount off the cover price. Many bookstores won't do business with a one- or two-book publisher, unless a customer specifically requests your book, because of the paperwork involved. Even then, the bookseller might tell the customer it can't find the book in its system. Before you get too huffy about the unfairness of it all, imagine for a moment that you're a bookseller and you have to set up a separate account for every book you stock or sell. What a nightmare. Instead, you'd want to order your stock not directly from thousands of publishers but from a handful of reputable wholesalers and distributors.

If a bookseller does agree to stock your title, it will probably expect the right to return any of your books that don't sell, at any time. Though general book business practices dictate that any returned book must be in salable condition, seasoned publishers will tell you that booksellers will return books regardless of whether the cover is scuffed, the pages are torn and dusty, or the spine is sticky with someone's spilled mocha latte. This is called selling on consignment. No, your book is not last season's moth-holed sweater or those pants that never fit right or that ugly pink top that you can just drop off at the resale shop without a care for its welfare. No matter, this is how the retail book industry operates. Selling books on consignment became a widely accepted business practice during the Depression, when publishers had to sell books that way or bookstores wouldn't take them at all. The method stuck and still dominates bookselling today. As for payment, expect it in 120 days. Or later.

"Consignment sales are almost unheard of in other industries, because most manufacturers know that without incentives to control inventory, retailers will order too much of whatever they're selling," says Chris Charuhas, president of Visibooks, a computer book publisher in Richmond, Virginia. "This has happened in the book business, where almost 40% of the books shipped to stores get shipped back to publishers, at the publisher's expense."

So, as you can begin to see, when it comes to retail bookselling, the power rests with the booksellers, distributors, and wholesalers and not with publishers—especially not with small publishers. Unless you have a best seller, what do you have to bargain with in your dealings with book retailers except your discount schedule?

"As a consequence, [publishers] have gradually ceded discount points, accommodated more returns, and found it increasingly difficult to enforce the rule that a returned book must be in resalable condition to receive credit," writes David Cole in his book *The Complete Guide to Book Marketing*. "Thus, publishers that depend on bookstores for the major portion of their sales need a higher sales volume to make a book profitable. At the same time, they need to make tighter budgets fuel stronger marketing because of the more competitive marketplace. This squeeze is especially hard on small publishers that have little margin for error and lack the economy of scale found in big houses."

Big publishers can afford to toss their returned books into a giant shredder and hire unionized truck drivers to haul the whole mangled mess to a recycle center, because their unit cost on each book is so much less than it is for small publishers. A standard print run for a big publisher might be twenty-five thousand copies. Small publishers go to press sometimes for a run of only five hundred copies, which makes the unit cost per book much, much higher. At such rates for books, you will find out very quickly that you don't have the luxury of throwing books away. Or, if you think you do, you'll go out of business.

"It is necessary constantly to remind yourself that when you have sold a book to a store, it's not fully sold," wrote Nick Weir Williams, in an article for the PMA newsletter. "It needs to be on someone's private bookshelf before that's true. And when you sell a book to a wholesaler, it's even less sold than it was when you sold it to the store. Unless it's a specific customer order, you've really only transferred it from your warehouse to someone else's warehouse."

Howard Fisher, publisher of Fisher Books and a past president of PMA, cites this Murphy's Law of Publishing: "Your largest return will most certainly arrive the same day as that big, optimistic second printing you ordered. Maybe even on the same truck!"

For the more literary publishers, whose first motivation in publishing books is to enlighten and enchant readers with poetry, or fiction, or literature, the state of book retailing today can seem corporate and cold. The more naive among them may long for the bookstores of yore, where store owners had all day to chat with customers about the lives of famous authors or a new work by a talented unknown.

OK, so for all these reasons it would be understandable if small publishers ignored bookstores. Except that you're probably feeling like you've done the hard part—you've written the book—and now you'd like just a little bit of the glamour that you thought went along with being a published (even a self-published) author. That means having your book on the shelves in bookstores. Right next to books by John Grisham and Maya Angelou and Dr. Spock and Martha Stewart. And not just your local bookstore. Nope, you want your book to be stocked in bookstores in cities where you've never even been and might not ever go. In your Aunt Bonnie's local bookstore; your high school boyfriend, Kurt's, local bookstore; your college roommate, Suzy's, local bookstore; and your professional rival's local bookstore, too. That, in part, is one of the reasons you wrote and/or published the book in the first place, right?

We would never advise you to keep your book out of bookstores. On the contrary, for many independent publishers, bookstore sales are an important revenue stream. Bookstores can also be the site of satisfying publicity efforts such as book signings, readings, and community events. Working with bookstore owners can give writers and publishers the opportunity to interact with their readers, and having your book on the bookshelf in bookstores sometimes offers the cache creative people and writers are often hungry for. If you've built up a relationship with a few bookstores and your book really starts to sell because of a choice publicity opportunity—say you get interviewed on the *Today Show* or land a spot on NPR's *Fresh Air* with Terry Gross—the somewhat complex system that arranges for books to get from your garage, storage facility, or printer and into the bookstores where people will be asking for them will already be in place. Trying to put such a system together on the fly is just about impossible and can cost you valuable sales.

Dan Poynter, the same guy who said bookstores are the worst place to sell books, recommends that small and independent publishers "tolerate bookstores" instead of going out of their way to make traditional bookstores the central source of their sales.

So, then, how does a small publisher go about "tolerating" bookstores? First, by starting local. Build a relationship with your local booksellers. You already are a good customer, right? If not, become one. Today. Booksellers will be much more receptive to a regular customer who asks whether the store would be interested in stocking his or her new book than to a complete stranger.

Communicate your enthusiasm about your book, and, if it's good, booksellers will get behind it. Even though in the beginning you may not be winning over a whole chain of bookstores or a whole network of independents, there are a lot of things individual booksellers can do for you.

For example, booksellers like to have events, because events get people into the store and sell books. Smaller stores especially are always on the lookout for local authors willing to do readings and signings. At your local bookstore, where you've become a favorite customer, you should know whom to contact for a signing or event. At bookstores further afield, visit the store's website to see whether the store is a good fit for you and whom you should contact.

Once you're on the store's calendar, ask for its media list and offer to help promote the event. The publicity budget for a bookstore, especially an independent bookstore, is probably as tight as yours, so anything you can do to help will be appreciated. Even if you sell only a few books at the actual event, a supportive bookseller can sell many more in the weeks after your visit. Any autographed books that don't sell can be advertised on the bookstore's website, if it has one. If these sell out, ask to do a "drop-by" signing. A drop-by signing is just what it sounds like: an author drops by a bookstore and signs stock. Unlike a scheduled book-signing event, no one is going to line up to purchase one of the books you or your author just signed, but the bookstore can offer a signed copy to customers in the coming weeks. Add a sticker to the cover that says "signed copy" if you like.

"It's good to do drop-bys for three reasons," writes Lissa Warren in her book *The Savvy Author's Guide to Book Publicity*. "One, it's a chance to meet-and-greet the people who can hand-sell your book, mention it in their store newsletter or on their store's website, and make it a 'staff pick' (which can get it some extra good shelf space). Two, a book signed is a book sold, because bookstores can't return autographed copies. And three, stores will often sticker signed copies (which calls attention to them) and create displays or special signs for them. It's a great way to get your book off the shelf and onto a front table."

Don't forget to reciprocate. Mention the bookstore on your website and list it in press materials aimed at local media. Include store bookmarks or coupons in a local direct mail campaign aimed at consumers. That will not only help get people to the bookstore for your signings but also bring them in during the following days and weeks, which is sure to impress the bookstore staff.

Second, "tolerating" bookstores means making it easy for bookstores beyond your local area to stock your book or special order it if it is not a title they regularly keep on hand. The most effective way to do that is to have your book available through Ingram Book Company and Baker & Taylor. Ingram's primary customers are bookstores, while Baker & Taylor serves mostly libraries and some bookstores. Ingram has warehouses across the United States, at least one of which is within one-day UPS shipping of more than 90 percent of the country's twenty thousand bookstores.

> *... booksellers like to have events, because events get people into the store and sell books. [Be] ... willing to do readings and signings.*

Virtually every retail bookstore uses these two companies to supply regular stock (best sellers, backlist books that sell year after year, new releases from popular authors, books of regional interest, etc.) but also to fulfill special orders. Certainly in the beginning of your publishing program, and perhaps for a long time to come, as far as bookstore sales go, you will be relying on customers asking for your book at their local bookstore, and so for the very best response, your book needs to be available at one or both of these wholesalers.

Wholesalers are reactive rather than proactive, meaning that sales are consumer driven. They do not send salespeople to bookstores to hand-sell books, as distributors do. Wholesalers merely fulfill orders as they are placed by the bookstores. It is important, however, to have this channel into the bookstores because they prefer to order from a small number of trusted sources. If you think you may want to pursue one of the major wholesalers, you can learn more about Baker & Taylor Books at www.btol.com. Just remember that you will need to go through an approval process and they are getting very picky. Ingram Book Group can be found at www.ingrambook.com, but you must have ten or more titles to work with this company.

You might then think that a distributor is the way to break into national bookstore placement. Well, it is if you can convince one of them that you are going to be able to create demand on a large enough scale to justify the investment in your book. The distributor must believe that your marketing and promotional plan, along with your book, is worth its time and resources. Remember that a distributor actually will take some of your inventory, put you in its catalog, and go out and try to get bookstores to order your book. Not a small task given the number of books released every week. While national distributors have helped small publishers, it is not the place to lay your bet if you want to get into bookstores.

One independent publisher, McPherson and Co. of Kingston, New York, has developed a model program to work with independent booksellers in an effort to "beat the fat cats at their own game," according to publisher Bruce McPherson. "While independent publishers like McPherson and Co. provide books that make independent booksellers stand out in the crowd, we can also promote booksellers to their communities through direct mail and Internet technology. And booksellers can strengthen independent publishers by showcasing their productions to their most savvy customers, as well as by employing a more efficient ordering program."

McPherson's goal for the program, which he started in 2004, was to sign on one hundred independent bookstore partners—a least one bookstore in every state—dedicated, at least in part, to nurturing independently published literature. Each bookseller receives a listing on McPherson and Co.'s website (www.mcphersonco.com) with a telephone number for orders as well as a link to the store's website. McPherson also lists the bookseller partners in the publisher's seasonal print catalogs announcing new and backlist books. For their part, bookseller partners agree to order two copies of each new release at a 40 percent discount, plus shipping, fully returnable. A month prior to publication, the partners receive an e-mail from McPherson and Co. containing a complete description of the new title and a cover graphic for use on the bookseller's website. For all titles, partners have the option of declining any particular book or expanding the size of their order.

Currently, McPherson has signed up an impressive list of partners, including the Tattered Cover in Denver, City Lights in San Francisco, and Harvard Book Store in Cambridge, among others.

Even though McPherson and Co. has been in business since 1974, has had more than twenty-five of its titles reviewed in *The New York Times*, and receives regular review coverage by *Publishers Weekly* and *Library Journal*, traditional bookstore distribution methods have been disappointing, McPherson said.

"We were one of Consortium's first publishers," he said. "After that, we fielded repping groups nationwide. But it never worked as well in practice as it did on paper. I'd never have developed a new program if our distribution had not become increasingly spotty as some of our better bookstores went out of business."

If you're inspired to establish a similar program with booksellers for your publishing company, keep in mind that McPherson traded on the relationships he has built up during his more than thirty years in the business and has chosen to work with independents over the chains. Chain booksellers can still order his titles, but he has not invited any of them to participate in his partners program.

"My relation with the chains has always been a little, shall we say, cautious," said McPherson. "B & N wouldn't buy when I was absolutely nonreturnable; now, they buy a little. At least so far."

Another way that independent publishers have tried to "tolerate" the retail bookstore market is to eschew master distributors in favor of using independent publisher representatives. At one time also called "travelers" or "territory managers," independent publisher reps can play an important role in making an independent publisher's relationship with bookstores a helpful and profitable one. The reps work on commission, and their job is to show a publisher's list to bookstore buyers. Their value to an independent publisher is the personal relationships with booksellers they've built up and their acquired knowledge of the character and clientele of each store that they call on. Generally, independent reps have contracts with several different publishers who produce lists that complement, but not compete with, each other. Reps are generally eager to work with committed independent publishers these days, as their role with big publishers has decreased in recent years.

"The rep network was a fantastic resource," Ed Morrow, owner of Northshire Bookstore in Manchester, Vermont, told *Publishers Weekly*. "Culture seeds traveling around the country, spreading the word about books they became familiar with at sales meetings and from buyers who had already read a galley or knew something about the author. That kind of fertilization was invaluable, but it's withering on the vine at a fairly rapid pace."

There are many reasons for this: the centralized ordering of the chains, the closing of so many independent bookstores, and the convenience and economy of the Internet, telemarketing, and 1-800 numbers, for starters. The job itself is not easy, making for lots of turnover. Changes in the industry require reps to cover more territory and present more titles. Traveling the country, visiting bookstores, meeting booksellers, and talking about books sound glamorous, but to be good requires a special kind of person. "After you start to see the dirt in the rooms, traveling loses its romance," said Jason Gobble, *Publishers Weekly* Representative of the Year in 2004. But for all these reasons, most reps have independent publishers among their contracted clients, and for independent publishers, this can be an economical way to reach bookstores—having just one representative on staff could cost $100,000 annually, or even much more when you add up salary, benefits, and travel expenses. Commissioned reps typically receive 10 percent of the list price for books sold to a retail outlet and 5 percent for those sold to a wholesale outlet.

The process works like this: an independent publisher rep meets with a publisher's marketing staff in a conference, sometimes face-to-face, sometimes over the phone, or, for the adopters of technology, via the web. New and forthcoming titles are discussed, including author information, book summaries, and upcoming publicity. At the sales conferences of large publishers, only a few minutes are spent on all but the highest-profile books, and if the staff reps don't like the book cover or the title, they say so. If their objections are strong enough, changes are made, sometimes even in the book's content. Imagine an independent publisher taking such action! For better or worse, independence earns you decision-making rights. If a small publisher doesn't have a marketing staff or even a marketing manager, the rep meets with the publisher. The best reps will read the new books so they can more effectively pitch them to their retail accounts.

The reps then visit their accounts up to four times a year, contacting those in the farthest outlying areas by phone. For each title, they establish a "hook," or reader benefit, to use in the sale and support this by showing the book jacket, endorsements, a summary of the book, and interesting nuggets about the author. For fiction, they may compare the book to a successful title the bookseller is familiar with or, for nonfiction, tell why it is superior to other titles on the market. The rep then moves on to the next title or the next publisher's list. When the visit is finished, the rep takes orders, reviews the store's stock of backlist titles, and handles returns.

If there is a downside for independent publishers considering contracting with commissioned reps, it's that reps have been conditioned to concentrate on the front list and therefore may push new books and ignore the sales possibilities of a publisher's backlist, the backbone of an independent publisher's effort at profitability. Also, simply because they are so enthusiastic about their lines, reps may oversell a title, creating a flood of returns later. Both of these issues can be overcome if you hire the right rep for your company.

9

INDEPENDENT PUBLISHERS AND INDEPENDENT BOOKSELLERS

Working Together?

Tracy Taylor, manager of Elliott Bay Book Company in Seattle, called them "fill-in-the-gap" books in an article in *Bookselling This Week*. In large measure, that's what booksellers think of the offerings from small, independent, and self-publishers. Yes, that's right: you are the movie trailer, the palate cleanser, the Spackle in the big, blank wall. To them, anyway.

Now, of course, booksellers know more than anyone that there is the odd self-published best seller. Before he was published by Rodale, author Arthur Agatston was busy handing out to his patients the diet pamphlets he wrote and published himself. You know his work better by its current title, *The South Beach Diet*. The popular children's book *Hank the Cowdog* found its first audience through author John Erickson's own publisher, Maverick Books. Now he's published by Gulf Publishing. Another best seller for kids, *The Beanie Baby Handbook*, was self-published, and so was another successful children's book, *Time Stops for No Mouse*. Even a few books that English teachers across the country would consider "classics" were self-published, too. These include James Joyce's *Ulysses*,

Louis L'Amour's *Smoke from This Altar*, Beatrix Potter's *The Tale of Peter Rabbit*, and John James Audubon's *The Birds of America*.

Booksellers also know that those are the exceptions, not the rule. The rule, from their experience, is that self-published books sell a few hundred copies to family and friends and then sit on the shelf until they are returned. If they even can be returned. If the publisher/author has a distributor. That characterization isn't pretty, but it is accurate. Tess Gerritsen, a best-selling author of medical thrillers, wrote about her experience that illustrates this point on her blog, which you can find at www.tessgerritsen.com/blog.

"I was reminded of this at a booksigning at a Barnes and Noble in New Hampshire. After the signing, the events coordinator thanked me for being 'so easy to work with—unlike some other authors.'"

'But I would think that most authors are pretty nice,' I said.

"'Most are,' she said. 'But the self-published ones are horrible. Then she described an incident that had happened earlier that week. A local self-published author had requested that the store arrange a booksigning for him, and she had turned him down flat. Enraged, he'd thrown the book on the floor and asked: 'When the hell am I ever going to get a signing in this store?'

"'When pigs fly,' she'd snapped at him. The man couldn't accept the fact that their store almost never hosted signings by self-published authors—even if the author was local.

"'Why not?' I asked. 'Is it because of the quality of the books?'

"'That's only part of it,' she said. 'The real reason is that we can't return them.'"

Another former bookseller, Patrick Shawn Bagley, who responded to Gerritsen's blog, puts it like this: "Since I'm no longer on the retail end of the book biz, my main issue with vanity and subsidy presses is the lack of editorial input. Some of these books, of which their authors are so proud, are downright awful. Yes, there are exceptions to the rule … Walt Whitman, L. Frank Baum … blah, blah, blah. The sad fact is, a lot of these self-published books are just not worth reading or promoting."

So, you should know going into it that this is the attitude of many (not all) independent booksellers. No wonder there is no formal effort on the part of independent booksellers to work with independent publishers who are publishing their own books. "Independent" doesn't mean "partnership," remember? You're going it on your own for a reason, so by your very nature you like that idea. You like depending on yourself and making your own decisions. You like not having to deal with obnoxious people if you choose not to. The independent bookseller is just like you, except it's selling books instead of producing them. Don't be one of the obnoxious people it chooses not to deal with.

If the last small/self/independent publisher/author/speaker who approached the bookseller before you was goofy or angry or unbalanced, that is what the seller will see when you walk in the door. Some advice to help both yourself and your fellow publishers and authors who come after you: don't be that person. Don't be the person who argues. Don't be goofy or smell weird. Instead, be the person with clean fingernails who is well groomed and dresses and acts professionally. Be the person who is polite, introduces himself or herself with a smile and a handshake, the person who asks whether this is a good time to talk. Be the person who takes "no" for an answer, if that is indeed the answer, and who politely finds a different way to ask again in a couple weeks. And a couple weeks after that, if need be. We're not saying to lie down if you think both you and the bookseller will be happy with the result of having your book stocked in the store. We're saying be the person who runs a polite, happily determined literary revolution of one. Be that person and you will have a far greater chance of developing a working relationship with your local independent bookseller than you would if you were the temper tantrum person.

"Local" is your key word here. If you are an untried author, you will have a far greater chance of booking a signing or getting an independent bookseller to stock your new book if it's your hometown store. Besides, you're a customer there, right? Meet the owner; check out the mood of the store. Then, when you announce that you're an author and have a new book coming out, it's a customer asking the store to stock his or her book, not a stranger. By then, the store knows you're not "Obnoxious Person"; you're just "Customer with a Book Person."

Next, offer booksellers the same 40 percent discount they get from the big publishers. They're taking a chance on you by using even a few inches of shelf space for your unknown, untried, and maybe unusual book. Why would they give you more favorable terms than they give Stephen King's publisher? Or Anita Shreve's? Or Barack Obama's? The answer is they won't. If you don't have a distributor, don't have an account with Ingram or Baker & Taylor, then offer the books on consignment. You get paid only when they sell. That means less risk for the bookseller, more of a chance it might work with you.

Next, make sure they sell. You're the author and the publisher, and that's your job. If you can't sell books in your own town, how are you going to sell them where you're a complete stranger? Send postcards to your cousins, bribe your friends, talk to your mother's book club, but get those books to pass by the cash register. If you can do all this (And this is the fun part, remember? This is why you're in business for yourself), you've successfully completed one loop of working with an independent bookseller. Keep it up.

OK, now you've made the bookseller a few bucks, and if you're lucky, you've got an ally. You're in a good position to ask whether that store would know of any stores in the region—close enough to be colleagues but far enough away not to be competition—that you should look into working with. Listen to what the store has to say, take the advice, broaden your bookseller circle, and don't forget that you're now "Polite Person" again. You're probably not a customer at these stores in your region, but you're going in with a prized possession, a recommendation from your hometown bookseller, who is one of their own. Keep this up until you're taking your book across state lines and you will have begun a good relationship from one independent to another. And another.

10

SAFELY NAVIGATING AMAZON.COM

(and Other Online Booksellers)

Amazon: Roald Dahl's *BFG* (Big Friendly Giant) or Big Brother? Either way, you can't deny that Amazon is probably the best way to go (at least when you're getting started). We'll give you tips and tricks to help market and sell your book on Amazon and look at the other side of the coin for publishers who aren't quite on board with the huge e-tailer.

The Good: Exposure, Exposure, Exposure

Don't you just love Amazon? Great graphics, simple navigation, intuitive organization, and so many choices! The variety of books and other products that make the site great for shoppers is exactly the thing that independent publishers have to work against. Being a successful Amazon seller is all about exposure. How many times can you get the cover, description, and ordering information in front of a customer while he or she visits the site?

"You need to expose your book to as many eyeballs as possible, which means that as many people as possible should see the detailed product description page for your book," wrote Brent Sampson, in the PMA newsletter. "The more visits to your description page, the better your book is going to perform. Simply put, the Amazon algorithm favors the most popular items, so if two different products match a user's criteria, the more popular one will show up first."

Amazon answers first to its customers and next to its suppliers. The site was originally designed and has been continually tinkered with to give its customers an incredibly detailed and personally tailored shopping experience. For example, when you visit the site, you see the "New for You" and the "Recommendations for You" lists of products right on the home page.

While these categories are listed at the top of the site as "your," the key implied word in all of those activities and choices is "my." Amazon has used your shopping history, along with any reviews you've written, lists you've made, or just pages you've looked at, to encourage you to feel some ownership in the site, and if you feel that, you'll come back again and again, not just to browse but also to buy.

Once you get past the spookiness of it, as a customer it feels good to know the site is working so hard to show you products you're probably interested in. As an independent publisher, it should feel good, too, says Sampson. "Because each user's shopping preferences are stored in its memory, Amazon can make sure that the people who see your book are likely to be interested in it."

So, how do you get that all-important exposure on Amazon.com? Here are a few good ways.

First, plug in to what the book portion of the site is known for—reviews. Be aware that some professional book critics have repeatedly ranted that online reviews by amateurs are meaningless. For example, in London's *Sunday Telegraph*, critic John Sutherland declared that Amazon reviews were leading to "the degradation of literary taste."

"Why do the web-reviewers allow themselves to be recruited as unpaid hacks?" he wrote in his column. "Partly for freebies. But more because they enjoy shooting off their mouths."

Such nastiness is best ignored, especially since it's just plain wrong. Yes, many of the reviewers on Amazon are amateurs, but that doesn't mean they don't know what they like and don't like about a book and how to communicate their opinions to potential readers—your potential readers.

Start out by researching reviewers who have posted well-written, considered reviews of books similar to yours. If you respect the way they review, send them an e-mail politely asking whether they'd be interested in reviewing your book on Amazon. Offer to send them a review copy. In your research, you're bound to happen upon Amazon's top reviewers, the ones who have posted hundreds and even thousands of book reviews on the site.

When you click on their profiles, they may even have a review policy and an address listed. If you can get one of the top ten, top fifty, or even top one hundred reviewers to post a review of your book, especially if it's a positive review that other people on Amazon deem helpful, it can be great for sales. These reviewers have a whole network of contacts and a whole bunch of cache with regular Amazon shoppers.

Make your contact with potential Amazon reviewers brief, and offer them a complimentary copy to consider for a review, but don't make them feel obligated. And, never ask for the book back—an amateur move, for sure. If they do write a review, make sure to send them a follow-up thank-you e-mail. Almost no one thinks to do this, or if someone does mean to, he or she doesn't follow through.

After you've made contact with people who already review on Amazon, ask your friends and family members to post a review—if they've read and liked the book, of course. A phony write-up shows and is worse than no review at all. You can also ask anyone you meet at a book signing, anyone who sends you a nice note, anyone who sends you an e-mail praising your book to post their thoughts on Amazon.

If you have received a review in any of the major trade or consumer print review outlets, Amazon may post them to your book's page. Amazon licenses these reviews directly from the media company that first published them. That's why you see

Publishers Weekly, The New York Times, and other reviews posted for some books. If you've received a review in one of these publications and it's not posted on your page, post it yourself. If you've received a print review in a small publication that doesn't license its reviews to Amazon, condense the review (Amazon allows only twenty words for these) and post it to your page, too.

Don't freak if someone posts a negative review. Read it, consider what the poster has to say, and then move on. Think of it as a right of passage. Writing and publishing are public acts. You're not really an author or publisher until someone takes a swipe at you. When it happens, consider yourself baptized in the Amazon. If, however, the review is entirely inaccurate or posted by someone who clearly has an ax to grind, contact Amazon and it may be removed. It's in Amazon's best interest to sell books, not to be a platform for angry posters.

Probably the first thing you filled out when you listed your book on Amazon was its detail page. Now that you've roamed all over the site and read the pages of other books, take a new look at yours. Make sure you've posted complete information and that your product description reads more like a movie trailer and less like an instruction manual. Even if your book is an instruction manual, you still want the description to read as compellingly as possible. This might be your only spot to catch a reader.

Next, check out Amazon's Co-Op Advertising opportunities, or its "Buy X, Get Y." For a fee you can pair your book with a hot seller. As a customer, this is the "Better Together" link you're likely to see made available to you when you click on a book you're interested in. This can cost $1,000 a month or more, and you have to submit your order between one and three months prior to when you want it to take effect, but if there is a hot-selling title that you think would be perfect bundled with your book, it may be worth considering. After you e-mail Amazon with a pairing request, you'll be sent specific pricing information and you can make a final decision then. Sending the request doesn't obligate you to participate, and there is no charge for the request itself.

Now that you've covered the basics as a publisher, start acting like a regular Amazon customer to make even more online friends and, hopefully, influence even more people to buy your book. The first place to start is by making a list. But before you make a list, you have to have an author profile. Create one by opening the page to your book and clicking on "I'm the author of this book." Now to the lists.

Browse Amazon and click on a book title that is in the same category as your book. Scroll to the bottom of the page, and there you will see Listmania. For example, I clicked on the book *The Wild Trees* by Richard Preston. Under Listmania the first list that popped up was titled "Read until Dawn" by someone I had never heard of but who was obviously an avid Amazon customer. When I clicked on the link, it took me to fifty books she thought would keep me up until dawn. When I clicked on her name, it took me to her profile, and I see that she is from Florida and has written three reviews and two lists. I can add her to my list of interesting people, invite her as an Amazon friend, or e-mail the page to anyone I'd like. There's also a link to make my own list. So, get busy and make your own list, but don't forget to add your book to it! Not at the top—that's too disingenuous—and not at the bottom, either, but somewhere north of the middle. Make sure the other books on your list are books that you endorse, that a reader of your book would be interested in, too. You can make as many lists as you'd like, each highlighting a different quality of your book.

Other opportunities to market on Amazon include the "Marketplace," where others can sell your book, "Tags" to identify information inside your book, and "Search Inside" to present excerpts of your book. Get to know Amazon, its nooks and crannies, and give these opportunities a try. You'll quickly identify which ones you're comfortable using and which ones increase sales.

The Scary: Working with a Powerful Big-Name Retailer

Although Amazon has a lot to offer, there can also be some drawbacks. The biggest worry these days is that Amazon takes too much money from the sale, something we touched on in the e-book pricing chapter. When it comes to e-books (and traditional print books), Amazon certainly places pressure on pricing, whether it's through royalty rates or by offering so many comparisons at lower prices. For example, if you were looking for a cookbook with vegetarian recipes, would you pick one priced at $24.95 or $5.99, all other factors equal? Yeah, that's what we thought. Consumers, competitors, and even Amazon itself can dictate the demand for lower-priced books.

Many independent publishers and authors worry about the influence that this all-powerful middleman can have when it is selling our books. Luckily, the fear of a "Great Depression" of e-book sales is far from being realized. "I see Amazon as a sort of ally," says Chad Post of Open Letter books. "There are probably only 250–300 physical bookstores carrying our books in the U.S., which would severely limit our potential readers if it weren't for an online retailer like Amazon. In terms of distribution and reaching as large an audience as possible, online retailers are fantastic for small presses."

John Oakes of OR Books isn't quite sold on Amazon's integral position in the online book market. "For us, Amazon is an occasionally necessary evil," he admits. "We started out *not* selling on Amazon, but we realized that a lot of people, after they read or hear about a book, go straight to Amazon. We are trying to slowly erode that mentality; it is just as easy to look up a book on a publisher's site as it is to look it up on Amazon."

With authors such as John Locke (who broke into the Kindle million-sellers club selling books at 99 cents a piece) utilizing Amazon to the fullest, we also have authors and publishers doing their own thing. Case in point: in 2011, superstar J. K. Rowling decided to sell her e-books on her own. "She didn't ask my opinion," Oakes jokes, "but Rowling and I are thinking the same thing.

She's found that she doesn't need Amazon to sell books and neither do other publishers." Oakes maintains that breaking consumers of the Amazon addiction will allow publishers to have direct contact with their readers. "It is an incredibly exciting time to be a publisher and to get in touch with your consumers. It is also a frustrating time because consumers don't understand they don't need to go through intermediaries to buy books."

Oakes makes a good point here. Why sell on Amazon if you can sell on your own site? Well, for one, Amazon (or other giants such as Barnes & Noble) is often the go-to for book searches. Readers are more likely to know the title or author of a work than they are to know the publisher, which limits your ability to sell from a personal or publisher website. At the moment, we're not very close to reaching Oakes's utopia of selling directly to readers, and it is both prudent and necessary to take advantage of Amazon opportunities. This should not, however, preclude you from selling books from your own site. As we'll discuss in the next chapter, consumers should be able to click on a "Buy This Book" link on your website, even if it only takes them to Amazon (preferably, it would not).

All in all, Amazon is the easiest and most visited site on which to sell your book. By all means, keep your options open and try to get your books sold through various different media. But, as almost any author will tell you, Amazon is too big a piece to ignore. So list your book a month or two before it's published (presales are always nice) and get to work on being invested and in tune with the Amazon community.

Other Places to Sell

The other two big players in the online business are B&N and the iBookstore. While you don't need to list your book on all three sites, it definitely can't hurt. Barnes & Noble functions quite similarly to Amazon and is the home of the Nook, a very popular e-reader. Just as on Amazon, you can list a print book or an e-book (B&N uses EPUB e-book format). The iBookstore delivers e-books to iPad, iPod touch, and iPhone users (also in EPUB format). Listing your book on Amazon is a necessity, and if you have the time and inclination, getting the trifecta of the online world is the best way to go.

Building Your Website

Be Google Ready

Before you even finish your manuscript, your website should be in the works. Nothing looks worse to a publisher, customer, or reviewer than typing your name into Google and coming up with … nothing. In this day and age, you can't afford the luxury of not being online. I'm not saying you need to sign up for Facebook, Twitter, LinkedIn, Google+, and every other social media site known to mankind (not yet, at least—I'll tell you to do that in a few chapters). Of course, you can do just that, and if you network and market properly, being super connected can be incredibly beneficial.

But, for the sake of simplicity, let's just stick with the basics. With the previous chapter in mind, it's quite clear that listing your book on Amazon is an obvious choice. We also suggest creating a personal website so readers can have a more direct link to you and your book. Having your own website will help you make direct sales, have contact with your customers, and, above all, maximize your profits.

There are two choices when it comes to creating your website: hire a pro or do it yourself. This decision all depends on your level of comfort with technology, as well as the amount of time and money you have available.

Hire a Pro (or at Least Get Some Advice)

If you still don't own a computer or are running an ancient dial-up beast, perhaps getting online will be tricky for you to do alone. Even if you're an experienced surfer, a professional web designer can give you the edge that you couldn't get if you created a site yourself.

"Professionals tend to stay more current with technology trends as well as coding standards and search engine algorithms," says Jon Roth, web strategist and developer. "As an author, your goal is to reach as many interested viewers with your web content as quickly as possible. Without a current, professional understanding of how websites optimally function, it's easy to make mistakes that inhibit that goal. You know 'what' you want to say to your audience, but slight differences in 'how' you say it and present it can make large differences in the effectiveness of your site. For example: how you structure the navigation and separate your content among pages can alter how search engines rank your site and how users experience your site. Additionally, attention to the structural details of each page, post, or discreet information area can make a significant difference to the traffic levels you ultimately attain."

Whom do I choose?

There are literally thousands of web developers and designers out there, so which do you choose? Again, it's time to do some digging and research several different options based on your needs. You can go local if you live in a large enough area, work through your publisher, or find someone else through the web. As always, ask for recommendations and examples of work. Look for a commerce-oriented web designer, someone who has had experience creating websites for product sales or, even better, other small publishers or authors.

There are two other important factors when looking for a web developer: years in the business and responsiveness. You'll want to hire someone who has had experience with web design and has passed the test of time. If your designer has been working on the web for ten years, it's likely he or she has been successful and will stick around to offer you support. In regard to responsiveness, your web developer should get back to you in a reasonable period of time when you have questions or request changes. These two requirements will ensure that your developer will stick with your project and give you the help and guidance that you need.

What Does a Developer Do?

If you choose to hire a web developer, he or she will help you get your domain name, create your layout, set up pages and options such as PayPal or Google Checkout, and make your site polished and easy to navigate. If you feel uncomfortable writing the copy for your website (e.g., the "About the Author" section), you can also hire someone in marketing to write or help you write the content of your site. Typical copywriters cost about $1 per word.

What Does It Cost?

A good web developer usually charges between $1,200 and $2,400 to build a site. This price all depends on your design needs and how complex you want your site to be. Remember that it will be well worth your money when the site is up and running and you're selling books by the bushel due to the great layout and convenience of your page.

Do It Yourself

If this isn't your first website (let's say you have a blog or have had a website in the past), there are a few simple steps to follow to make sure your website will be tailored to selling you and selling your book. You should feel comfortable on the web, navigating pages, and filling in forms. If you're experimenting with web design for the first time, pay close attention.

Step One: Domain Name

Domain names are relatively easy to come by these days. Companies such as Go Daddy (godaddy.com) can set you up with a domain name for a small fee and very little hassle. Try to keep your URL simple and easy to remember and skip awkward characters such as asterisks or plus signs. If you're planning on writing more than one book (and don't want to create multiple websites), consider using your name or your publishing company's name as the URL.

Step Two: Choose a Template

Go Daddy and similar third-party sites (such as buildyourwebsite.com) give you thousands of layout options. Look for one that has good contrast between the background and the text (navy blue on black isn't the easiest to read), uses a clear font, and offers a simple but classic design. You can certainly get creative with your layout, but steer clear of pages that are too cluttered (or sparse), confusing for visitors, or overly psychedelic (go easy on the neon, tie-dye, and rotating backgrounds).

Step Three: Create Your Pages

Here are some basic pages that you will need on your site:

- **Home page:** This page includes basic info about you and your book, perhaps a couple of photos, recent news, and links to other sites. This should have well-written copy to drive interest for first-time visitors.
- **About the Author:** If you don't already have a biography, start writing one. As we mentioned earlier, you can also get some outside help when writing your website copy. Your site is one giant PR piece, and you want it to be as nice as possible. If you feel uncomfortable blatantly promoting yourself, get someone else to do it for you. On this page, you should include information about your background, your experience with writing, your related interests, etc.
- **Merchandise/Purchase page:** This is where you will have your books or any other merchandise available for your readers. We'll go into more detail on this page in a minute.
- **Media section:** Upload all of your positive reviews, newspaper mentions, awards, or achievements

related to your book. Again, it's shameless promotion, but it's necessary.
- **News/Events:** Be sure to keep this section up to date. Include book signings, release dates, TV or radio appearances, etc.
- **Contact:** Give your readers a way to contact you with fan mail or questions. You don't need to provide the direct route to your front door, but give them a phone number, e-mail address, or P.O. box (or all three!).
- You can also include an "About the Publisher" section, a page for each of your books, and/or a "Sample Content" page where visitors can read an excerpt or download a chapter for free.

Roth suggested doing targeted keyword research. "This way, you know which terms relevant to your topic areas are generating the best search traffic. Then plan your site content around those terms, but be sure to design your narrative and navigation to be as user friendly as you can. At the end of the day, conversions come from a good user experience."

Step Four: Merchandise Setup

Because you're selling a book, you'll need a website merchant payment function such as PayPal or Google Checkout. Wait to create a shopping cart center; these can be complex and sometimes expensive and are really necessary only when you have a large inventory of products (we're talking fifty different items).

Step Five: Marketing

Once your website is up, it's time to get the word out. Start linking to your site in every Facebook post and tweet, and add it to your e-mail signature. Put it on bookmarks and in any of your promotional material, and ask your friends to promote it, too. As for search engine optimization, submit your URL to Google to help it move up in the ranks. Search engines such as Google try to provide the most readily accessed sites with the best content, and this should be you.

Step Six: Editing

Oh, yes, the editorial process does not end with your final manuscript. Readers will be just as disappointed if they find typos on your website. You can have your editor briefly look over your site or just enlist a small army of friends and acquaintances to play around with it. Have them look for errors but also gauge the ease with which they can navigate the page. You want all of your pertinent information front and center, with simple one-click options to get where visitors want to go.

Extra Tips

If you're really feeling ambitious, you can create extra sites for each of your books or projects. Make sure that you link these back to your home site. Also include links to any blogs, columns, or other places where readers can get more of your writing. You can also link to your publisher.

Some publishing companies and service firms will connect you to web templates that are especially good for authors and publishers. These layouts have all the features you will need and won't bog you down with random details or pages. For a good example, check out YourPubSite.com.

Roth had a few more suggestions for author websites:

- Research sites that inspire you and that appear to be popular with the audience to which you would like to appeal. Notice the features, interface design, and storyline that these sites use and consider how similar approaches might suit your mission.
- Frequent sites where your audience congregates and listen to what they say there by reading comments or forum posts. Participate in conversations online.
- Identify what you think are the top issues within the community and then design your site to address

those issues specifically. Be sure to include features (such as a blog built into your site or a link to a blog you maintain on a popular blogging platform) that encourage participation from your audience.

- All roads should lead back to your book(s) and to the writing you do on your topics. Your website should be an extension of the narratives in your books as well as an open door for your audience to interact with you.

12

PRINT-ON-DEMAND

A Way In, Not a Way Around

Print-on-demand (POD) started out with a bad rep. At the turn of the century, we were bombarded by catch lines such as:

"Take the mystery out of achieving publishing success!"

"We put our trust in the big league of unknown authors!"

"Great publishing is a Great Adventure!"

And, our personal favorite,

"We're fast. Super-mega-crazy fast! You can publish and order within minutes!"

This type of propaganda, especially in the case of the latter example, didn't really live up to the hype. Print-on-demand is not a new kind of publisher but rather a relatively new kind of printing technology. It enables publishers and authors to print one book at a time.

Revolutionary in itself, yes, considering that traditional offset printing requires a minimum run of five hundred to one thousand copies just for the publisher to break even, but remember that POD doesn't take that unpublished novel in your underwear drawer and turn it into a best seller, it doesn't get you on TV, it doesn't get your memoir reviewed in *The New York Times Book Review*, and it doesn't stock your travel guide face out by the bookstore cash register. Sorry, only you, and your writing and marketing talent and ambition, can do that, not a piece of machinery.

"Not only has traditional publishing not been revolutionized, or even much affected, POD's position in the publishing universe remains suspect, even disreputable to some," wrote senior editor Sean Wallace, of Prime Books, in *Locus Online* in 2004. "The reasons for POD's failure to achieve its revolution are varied, but much of the blame and stigma is a consequence of the first ecological niche that was available for it to occupy: vanity publishing."

That's right: the entrenched, elitist, change-resistant, inefficient, perplexing, and maddening business we call publishing began by viewing most new POD releases as vanity press books—and there is no bigger lock on the door to that room marked "Successful Published Author" than the one that denies entry to authors whose books are published by vanity presses.

Companies such as AuthorSolutions, PublishAmerica, Lulu, and others may bill themselves as publishers, but they are really service providers to authors. Some critics in the industry even call them "author mills," a term reminiscent of the mistreated, innocent, and doomed puppies bred by heartless "puppy mill" breeders interested only in making money off their pedigree.

Think about it this way: book publishers make their money selling books to readers; author mills make their money selling services to authors. During POD's early years, some of those services were suspect in quality and drastically overpriced. For example, in 2003 more than 130 writers petitioned the Maryland attorney general to investigate a POD service provider, PublishAmerica, because they said that, despite all claims to the contrary and the token $1 advance promised in the publishing contract, the publisher is a vanity press and will accept virtually any manuscript. As proof, the writers pointed to a phony manuscript submitted by Arizona writer Dee Power that repeated the same ten pages eight times and mixed up the main characters' first names.

In another example, a group of member writers of Science Fiction Writers of America became irked when PublishAmeria staff criticized the quality of science fiction writing as a genre on one of its websites. "As a rule of thumb, the quality bar for sci-fi and fantasy is a lot lower than for all other fiction … [Sci-fi authors] have no clue about what it is to write real-life stories, and how to find them a home." The site went on to describe these genre writers as those "who erroneously believe that Sci-fi, because it is set in a distant future, does not require believable storylines, or that Fantasy, because it is set in conditions that have never existed, does not need believable every-day characters."

As you can imagine, that didn't go over too well with the Science Fiction Writers of America. Thirty of them were incensed enough to test the quality control at PublishAmerica by submitting what they called the "absolute worst book ever written." The manuscript, *Atlanta Nights* by Travis Tea, was thrown together in a weekend, with each writer contributing a chapter, and was submitted to PublishAmerica, which agreed to publish it. In January of 2003, the group of writers revealed that the submission was a hoax, and PublishAmerica immediately announced it was withdrawing its offer.

Now, many of these horror stories and warnings don't apply to you. Why? Because you have already invested in services that the writers above did not: professional editing and interior design. While we can never guarantee a book's success, we can promise that a well-written, good-looking book will do a hell of a lot better on the market than something such as *Atlanta Nights*. Many authors made the mistake of believing POD could replace all of the services of a traditional publisher, which is not the case. POD has a lot of benefits, both environmentally and cost-wise, but you still have a bit of legwork to do before going to print.

When POD companies first started appearing more than a decade ago, the process was not as fine-tuned as it is now. Today, POD has really turned its image around; instead of providing an outlet for anyone and anything to get published, POD service providers are looking more closely at manuscripts and are infinitely more accurate in their promises of success (and, for the most part, POD services no longer call themselves publishers).

Many publishers and university presses make use of POD technology for reprints, backlists, and test marketing. While the stigma of a vanity press still hovers over POD (and, admittedly, its primary use does seem to be along these lines), many big names in the industry have started their own POD companies. For example, Lightning Source is a division of Ingram, Create Space is an Amazon company, and Replica Books belongs to Baker & Taylor.

OR Books is infamous for its use of POD publishing. "We came from traditional publishing," publisher John Oakes says. "When we started, we were still setting a print run and ordering copies. Inevitably we'd miscalculate and end up with a lot of copies sitting in the warehouse. Now we work with BookMobile out of Minnesota and have had very good experiences that we are only looking to continue. They have been very interested in our model of selling direct and are environmentally friendly, which is very important." BookMobile has been in business since 1982, uses 30 percent recycled paper in its printing, and is a wind-powered company, which only adds to its sterling reputation. "We no longer have to guess how many books to print, pay warehousing fees, or worry about inventory," Oakes says. "Per unit it costs more, but in the long run it is cheaper because if you do POD, you only print as you need the book so the consumer has already paid and the publisher doesn't lose money." Oakes also raves about the ability to eliminate a middleman and create real relationships between customer and publisher.

Many publishers, whether or not they use POD services, will recommend it to other authors and smaller houses, assuming you have the right kinds of books and it suits your needs. That is, POD is a great solution to reduce inventory, keep tighter control over costs, and make sure that revenue is not locked up in inventory. There are a lot of solutions out there for this sort of thing as well, so you only have to ask around to find the right fit.

Using the right POD technology can provide you with an inexpensive, but still high-quality, entry into the publishing market. Unfortunately, there are at least a hundred companies out there trying to push you through a door you are probably completely capable of walking through all by yourself. With your shirt still firmly on your back, no less. So, let's take a look at how print-on-demand technology is being sold to naive authors as a "way around" the traditional gatekeepers of the publishing industry and how it is being used as a viable way into the market by self-publishers and established independent publishers.

First, the "way around." The POD service providers that have captured the attention of inexperienced authors and subsequently have flooded the market with books can be divided into two general categories: those that charge an author a fee to publish his or her book and those that don't. Initially, you might think that the fee-charging POD service providers are the bottom rung, with those service providers offering to publish your book for "free" a step above. Of course, all writers have been told that they should never have to pay to get published, and most mainstream publishers, booksellers, and reviewers continue to adhere to that truism. Well, it's become a little more complicated than that. Remember when your mother said, "Never say 'never'"? Of course, we're assuming here that you are comparing the two out of intellectual curiosity and not because you are considering actually using their services, right? Right.

> *... publishing needs to be professional, and professional rarely means free.*

OK, while POD service providers that charge authors a fee are immediately labeled vanity presses by the industry, as a general rule, they do offer nonexclusive contracts, and they also give their author/clients a chance to terminate their contracts via written notice. This is unheard of from the non-fee-charging PODs. Fee-charging POD service providers also offer authors a higher royalty schedule.

POD service providers that don't charge a fee oftentimes lock their author/clients into ridiculously long contracts (seven years isn't unheard of), demand exclusive rights to sell the book, and offer teeny tiny royalties. Believe me, they may not charge you an upfront fee, but they're going to make their money somewhere. But whether one of these service providers charges their authors a fee isn't as important as you might think at the outset.

"Unfortunately, it is necessary to acknowledge the fact that the absence of a fee is far less relevant (for the time being, at least) than you would expect it to be," writes Clea Saul on BooksandTales.com, a website with a large amount of information about POD service providers. "A number of independent bookstores, and most major bookstore chains, refuse to carry POD published books and insist that they only deal with 'real' publishers."

If we've taught you anything so far, it's that publishing needs to be professional, and professional rarely means free. We're not saying you have to spend the next five years and $500,000 trying to get your title published by Random House, but we do advocate choosing the most trusted and proven services (keeping your budget in mind, of course). Before you get too excited about printing your book "for free," shop around. The Internet has thousands of reviews and recommendations for POD providers, and putting some faith in a "brand" name (such as those of Ingram or Amazon) is never a bad idea. If you're at a loss, you can also contact publishers or authors to see whom they use for POD or contact a POD service to see whether it has a list of popular clients or success stories.

13

BREAKING INTO INDIEBOUND

"Book Sense Evolved"

If you haven't heard of IndieBound, formerly Book Sense, you've either been working really hard on your book for the past, oh, thirteen years or else you're one of the very few people without access to any of the one thousand member bookstores in fifty states, Puerto Rico, Bermuda, and the Virgin Islands. Launched in 1999, Book Sense quickly became the crown jewel of the American Booksellers Association (ABA). The ABA is the trade group that has taken its mission, championing the role of the independent bookstore in our society, and turned it into an art form. Book Sense became IndieBound a few years back, with several updates (the ABA called IndieBound "Book Sense Evolved"). IndieBound has indeed given independent booksellers new power and identity, but in the meantime, the program has also given independent publishers rare access to buyers at those one thousand stores.

If you're reading this guide sequentially and not jumping around, you've recently read about why bookstores are the worst place for independent publishers to sell books. You've also read about why the obvious alliance that should exist between independent publishers and independent booksellers doesn't. Don't forget a single word of either one of those chapters, but temper all of that caution about selling your book in bookstores with what you're going to read here about IndieBound.

The ABA touts IndieBound as a "movement that extends beyond reading. Just as each town is special, the local businesses that serve that community provide for their constituents in a way that homogenized, international chain establishments never could. Whether you've found the perfect independent coffee shop, record store, hardware store, or other locally-owned business, IndieBound will help you get the word out."

What's the difference between the old Book Sense and the new IndieBound? The ABA says that "IndieBound takes Book Sense to the next level by empowering each member of the community to stand up and be proud. Love good books? Love sharing that passion with fellow readers? Love your local independent store? IndieBound celebrates the enthusiasm and energy of dedicated book fans and spreads the news. Both within the four walls of your favorite bookstore or outside them, IndieBound raises awareness of the inimitable and inestimable value of independent businesses."

When the ABA came up with the idea for Book Sense, it was a plan originally dominated by its online component to offer a way for independent booksellers, who couldn't otherwise afford an e-commerce website, to compete with online bookseller Amazon.com. By 1999, most of the superstore damage to independent bookselling had been done. In twenty-five years, the retail bookselling market share controlled by independent bookstores had dropped from 84 percent to about 17 percent. Hundreds of small, family-owned, and even medium-sized and large independent bookstores had gone out of business, while very few new independent stores opened to take their places.

Currently, www.booksense.com is still operable, but as an ABA member store locator, it is not a vehicle for e-commerce. "While Book Sense does have an online component, in-store marketing materials comprise most of the strategy's depth," writes Jennifer Boykin, a specialist in association management, in an article for Executive Update titled "Small Fish Survival Lesson." "Specialized services and marketing tools that can be customized help members compete while maintaining the fresh, fun, friendly edge not always possible with larger chains. Book Sense not only helps member stores address tough competition from Goliaths; it also has given the independent bookseller industry increased prestige in the minds of a key supplier—the publishing industry."

While IndieBound is being consistently fine-tuned by the ABA, its current components include:

- The Indie Next List: a list of independent bookseller recommendations printed on thousands of flyers handed out free in member bookstores.
- The Indie Best-Seller List: the favored titles from reporting independent bookstores across the country.
- National advertisements in magazines such as *The New Yorker*.
- www.IndieBound.com: consumer websites to publicize the IndieBound best-seller list and to help web surfers find an independent bookseller in their neighborhood, town, or city.
- www.IndieCommerce.com: the ABA's e-commerce product for independent bookstores, where ABA members can sell books and merchandise online.
- Indieessentials: monthly lists from ABA publisher partners of enduring titles that local indies love.
- Advance access to readers' copies from publishers.

This last component, advance access, is the most valuable one for independent publishers. Advance access invites publishers (of any size or persuasion) to offer free advance reading copies to independent booksellers, the idea being that once a bookseller sees how great your book is, it will want to place an order. Once a month, the IndieBound staff e-mails its member stores news of galleys, reading copies, or finished books that publishers are offering free for review. And every month stores then contact publishers directly via e-mail to request a copy of the books they want to take a look at and then decide whether to stock the title. Buyers may also nominate the book for a spot on the IndieBound best-seller list at this time. According to the ABA, publishers should anticipate between twenty-five and fifty requests from booksellers, but seventy or eighty is not unheard of. Booksellers know that the program is first-come, first-serve, but if you are not willing to part with at least twenty-five free copies, you can stop reading right here—and take a moment to reconsider.

To participate, send a description of your book to the Book Sense marketing director with the title, author, publisher, ISBN, subject category, publication date, number of free copies you have to offer, a two-sentence description (maximum), and a return e-mail address booksellers can write to and request a copy. The IndieBound staff is often very particular about the format, so follow the above instructions to the letter. Do not include any other information, such as website addresses or press releases or cover art. That kind of unwanted information would just gum up the process and get deleted, anyway. Due to the popularity of the program, the IndieBound staff cautions that it may take two to three weeks from the time you send your e-mail to receiving the information from the booksellers.

"There's no obligations or promises, but our program is one way to prime the pump and get the word out," said the program's founding director, Carl Lennertz, in a letter to the members of Publishers Marketing Association. "I feel passionately that Book Sense can be a real conduit from the independent publishers to the independent booksellers of deserving books with little or no marketing budgets. Every book deserves a chance!"

When you reply to the requests from a bookseller, that is the time to include press material and author information, along with a personal note thanking the bookseller for its interest and suggesting that if the store really enjoyed the book, it could nominate it to the

IndieBound best-seller list. While you're still in competition with the Random Houses and Doubledays and Knopfs of the publishing arena, your book is up for the task, right?

Another way for independent publishers to participate with IndieBound is through its Publisher Partner Program. Partnership is available to any publisher with at least five titles currently in print and readily available for booksellers to order either direct or from wholesalers.

Being a part of the Publisher Partner Program allows the option of a "Red Box" or "White Box" mailing kit. The boxes, measuring 18 1/2" × 18 1/2" × 4, are mailed straight to partners and stores and include tons of great bookseller materials. The "Red Box" reaches more than one thousand ABA member stores and offers publishers a fast way to get time-sensitive materials into the hands of booksellers. The ABA describes the Red Box as a monthly "In-Store Marketing Action Kit" that "contains the store's initial allotment of the latest Indie Next List flyers as well as any other timely news from ABA and IndieBound. Publishers may provide shelftalkers, easelbacks, bookmarks, posters, or other point-of-purchase materials to support titles chosen by booksellers as Indie Next List books, as well as other recent releases. Other enclosures may include seasonal catalogs, sell sheets and/or order forms for any off-the-list titles, special offers with specific deadlines, and other late-breaking news about titles, authors, tours, confirmed media appearances, etc."

The White Box is sent to 750 stores that "earn" the mailing through "their participation in various IndieBound and ABA initiatives each month—regular reporting to the Indie Bestseller List, nominating books to the Indie Next List, maintaining a permanent IndieBound in-store display, participating in the ABA IndieCommerce Program. Included in the White Box are galleys, Advance Reading Copies (ARC's), and finished books that booksellers read and consider stocking, handselling and nominating to the Indie Next Lists." Both the Red Box and the White Box are great opportunities for you to get information out to stores across the nation.

While savvy publishers will want their materials to be sent to stores that report sales to the best-seller lists, there are no such guarantees. In fact, most reporting stores are already visited by sales reps, who can supply them with galleys and promotional goodies, while the smaller, out-of-the-way, and hard-to-reach stores are the ones that really need, and get, the Red or White Box. The ABA and the IndieBound staff do allow Publisher Partners to specify which region of the country they want to concentrate on. Specifying regional distribution of materials in the box mailing is possible—so if, for example, the publisher has a title of interest in the Northeast or the Midwest, it could request that the IndieBound staff make sure the galleys go primarily to Northeast or Midwest member stores.

So, while there are no assurances that participating in the box mailing will improve a publisher's chances to get the book onto a best-seller list, IndieBound does monitor its member stores to make sure that they are active participants. Any bookstore that wants to receive the box mailings must fulfill two of the four following criteria: report to the best-seller list at least three weeks each month, send in at least one Indie Next List nomination each quarter, establish and maintain a permanent IndieBound display area in the store, and actively participate in the IndieBound gift card program. There are more than one thousand member stores, but the box mailing is sent only to those stores that meet participation criteria. To participate in the Publisher Partner program, go to www.IndieBound.com to fill out an e-mail with what you would like to send, what month, and any other specifics you have in mind.

Book Sense and IndieBound have worked well for some independently published books. There are hundreds of titles from small and independent publishers that have been a hit with booksellers and made the best-seller list. Examples include *The Coal Tattoo: A Novel* by Silas House (Algonquin); *How to Be Lost* by Amanda Eyre Ward (MacAdam/Cage); *Ordinary Wolves: A Novel* by Seth Kantner (Milkweed); *Call Girl* by Jeannette Angell (Permanent Press); *Owls and Other Fantasies: Poems and Essays* by Mary

Oliver (Beacon); *Ghosts in the Garden: Reflections on Memory, Identity, and Meaning* by Beth Kephart (New World Library); *The King's English: Adventures of an Independent Bookseller* by Betsy Burton (Gibbs Smith); *I Want My Dinner Now! Simple Meals for Busy Cooks* by Renee Pottle (Hestia's Hearth Publishing); *Job Hopper: The Checkered Career of a Down-Market Dilettante* by Ayun Halliday (Seal Press); and *Water for Elephants* by Sara Gruen (Algonquin Books).

I could go on, but you get the idea. One of the most unjust truisms of small-press publishing is that you have to break through a wall of prejudice to get to unbiased eyes. Agents, editors, reviewers, distributors, and sales reps all are well known for being predisposed against small publishers, but booksellers want to satisfy customers. Get your good book in front of booksellers and they don't care whether you're Random House or Raucous House—if they can sell it, they want to stock it and recommend it to their customers.

14

Managing the Mass Market

Discount Outlets

Here's a trivia question: What was the largest outlet for children's book sales every year since 2001? Answer: Discount stores such as Kmart, Walmart, and Target have captured nearly 30 percent of all children's book sales. Granted, the survey includes coloring book sales, but it's still impressive. These outlets represent enormous sales potential: a single best-seller book order can call for forty thousand copies or even more. Plus, you may reach an audience who might never see your book otherwise. Yet, this is one of the most difficult of all channels.

For your book to succeed, it must move off the shelf and into consumers' hands. If it doesn't, it is not advantageous for a small press to work with a discount store or mass merchandiser.

In general, these huge corporations typically take ninety days to pay and usually don't pay in full, retaining a certain fraction of the payment for potential returns. Also, these outlets are generally unwilling to negotiate a "no-returns" policy with new or small publishers.

Typically, publishers sell books to warehouse club distributors at a wholesale discount, generally between 55 and 60 percent. That compares favorably to national book distributors, who usually take a 63 percent discount or higher.

Although warehouse club sales are quite risky for one- to two-book publishers, there are ways of minimizing the chance of losses; for small publishers and unproven books, the publisher and warehouse club may agree to "test-market" a book by placing small quantities in ten or twenty regional stores. If a book does extremely well, the club will roll out the book nationally and order much higher quantities. If it doesn't, a couple thousand copies of the book found a home and everyone is happy.

This is an outlet publishers shouldn't attempt until their book (or books) has been proven a winner in terms of sales and publicity. There's simply too much to lose. Besides, these corporations usually "qualify" publishers in terms of how many books they publish, their credit history, and past sales success. Yet if your book has shown that it has wings and can fly off the shelves, go for it.

So how do you go about getting your book into these stores? The buying process among these outlets works like this: warehouse clubs and mass-merchandising stores buy their goods from distributors and rarely from publishers because of the handling costs involved.

Therefore, a lot of times a warehouse club buyer decides to buy a book on the recommendation of the distributor's rep. Other times, a publisher's rep has visited the warehouse club buyer and successfully persuaded him or her to buy a title (small publishers, however, don't have enough clout to get in to see a warehouse club buyer; it's even difficult for Simon & Schuster).

Finally, buyers of certain clubs will determine themselves that a given book would be a good buy after reading a great review, hearing about it from numerous friends, seeing it in a book trade show, or reading or hearing an author interview. If they want the book, they'll ask their distributor to get it for them.

As a publisher, you need to tackle these stores from both sides of the stream: the warehouse club or mass merchandiser's book-buying department and the distributor that serves them.

When ordering quantities, the book buyer determines whether it wants to offer the book as a "single SKU" (stock keeping unit) or as an assortment. A "single SKU" simply means that the book stands by itself. These books are typically the best-seller types. A small publisher's book is typically offered in an assortment display, meaning it's offered alongside books of similar size, price, and subject matter.

Therefore, it behooves a publisher to do the homework and suggest a specific assortment with all the respective publishers' names and contact numbers. Your book will get presented much faster, said the marketing director of a major distributor. For example, if you have published a regional cookbook, look up publishers of other regional cookbooks and ask whether they'd be willing to sell their book at Sam's Club or Target.

Some publishers balk at the thought of getting displayed side-by-side with their competition, believing it would drain sales away from their own book. In reality, the publisher may never get these sales in the first place since many warehouse club shoppers don't patronize bookstores.

Before trying to pitch your book to a distributor or a wholesale club or mass-merchandising store, be sure to make a few visits to the particular store to get an idea of what it offers.

Generally, these stores carry best sellers, but if you're a small publisher who publishes fiction, warehouse clubs will most likely be interested in stocking your titles if you have children's fiction. Well-illustrated books with a cute story do best. Young-adult selections can also sell well. You might also find regional-interest books and calendars from small publishers on the shelves.

A store visit allows you to determine whether your book fits in with the store's current book inventory, and you can also check on whether there's a fit between your book and a given department.

Tim Smith, for example, was able to get Meijer Inc., a Midwest chain of more than 150 "one-stop-shopping" centers, to stock his book, *Buck Wilder's Small Fry Fishing Guide*, in its outdoor department.

If you are convinced after your visit that your book could do well in a given store or warehouse club, call the store's corporate office and ask for the name of the appropriate book buyer.

Next, call the buyer and be ready to discuss, in just a few words, the book and its past sales successes in particular outlets. If the buyer seems interested, mail a book, cover letter, and hard evidence that the book will perform like a winner: sales performance in other outlets that would suggest success in a warehouse club, media appearances (past and future), book reviews, and a summation of your publicity campaign.

Selling to chain stores can be a terrific challenge. Jim Denardo, president of the Michigan sales firm Adventure Marketing, describes trying to sell Tim Smith's *Buck Wilder's Small Fry Fishing Guide* to Meijer Inc.

"Chains are not that easy. Meijer once told me they wanted the Buck Wilder book but that they couldn't buy it directly from me. I did a flip on that one," he said. "I had to sell it to another company, Faber Brothers, because it's the fishing distributor for Meijer's outdoor section. It's a tangled web. The whole industry is that way."

Denardo has learned that it takes persistence to get into major chains. After he makes contact with the right book buyer, he makes at least a dozen calls and sends several review copies before a sale is made.

Wade and Cheryl Hudson, owners of Just Us Books, found that persistence paid off when it came to getting into Toys "R" Us. Since the company was founded in 1998, Just Us Books has grown into a million-dollar-a-year publishing company.

Just Us Books is a publisher of Afrocentric children's books, so Wade first contacted the corporate office and asked for the name of the children's book buyer. He then sent five copies of previously published books with a cover letter. He made five or six calls just to rise above the noise of all the other titles the buyer received. He made four subsequent shipments of the five books, he said, just to get the company's attention. Finally, Toys "R" Us placed its first order for $36,000 worth of books.

To establish their company's credibility, the Hudsons placed a full-page ad in *Publishers Weekly* and also ran ads in *School Library Journal*, *The New York Times Book Review*, and other publications.

The ads were expensive, but they familiarized the buyers with the Just Us Books name, making it easier for the company to get in the door. The Hudsons eventually signed up with a distributor, which helped the firm get its books into other chains as well.

Is a warehouse club or mass merchandiser for you? If the fit is right, absolutely. The profit potential is enormous, but tread carefully. Be aware that some clubs and discount stores have specific requirements when it comes to pricing, so be sure you do your research and talk with store representatives (or authors who have used mass merchandisers) to make sure you have all the necessary information.

Section III
Promotion

"Perfecting and selling your writing is a lifelong task. If you are a persistent writer you can expect your abilities to improve with time. Success is the ability to go from failure to failure without losing your enthusiasm."
—WINSTON CHURCHILL

So you're finally ready to sell your book. You've put together a polished product and have chosen the perfect place, or places, to sell it. This section will get into the nitty-gritty of promotion, marketing, social media, and alternative sales platforms to help you get the most out of your book. When selling a house, you have the decision to hire a real estate agent or create your own listings. Similarly, we'll discuss the professional and do-it-yourself promotion opportunities and give you the tools to get your book into the hands of as many readers as possible.

15

DETERMINING YOUR MARKET

Who Wants to Read Your Book?

When you first started writing your book, your audience consisted of you and the inhabitants of your fish tank. The circle of trust expanded to let in your mom, your significant other, and a few of your closest (and least judgmental) friends. We made you push it out a bit further to include an editor, an interior designer, and some kind of publishing consultant.

It's time for the final push: every literate being who has access to a bookstore, computer, or telephone. In a perfect world, this would be your target audience, and your book would be beloved by all ages, genders, and nationalities. However, this is unlikely to be the case, which makes it all the more important that you define your audience and determine your market. Case in point: the Bible has sold more copies than any other book, ever. But do you see a Bible in every store you walk into or in every household you visit? Of course not. We'll keep it simple by using the classic five Ws (who, what, where, when, and why) to illustrate important audience and marketing points.

Who

Who wants to read your book?

These are the people you had in mind when you were writing your book. If your book is very specific (e.g., Floribunda Roses for the Gardening Enthusiast), your market should present itself quite clearly. However, if you're writing a piece of mainstream fiction or a thriller, there is a little more work to do. It's time for another comparative analysis. Look at the customer reviews for a book that is similar to yours on Amazon. Do the reviews come from men or women? Can you guess their age or demographics? What do they like about the book, and what bothered them? Use this information to develop a very clear picture of your audience; you want to create as much detail as possible.

Who needs to buy your book, and who wants to buy it?

There is a difference between these two. A new mother NEEDS to buy your book *The Definitive Guide to Motherhood*, whereas a reader WANTS to buy your latest novel about life in the Southwest. If your book does not lend itself to the "need" category (which makes book sales a whole lot easier), market it appropriately. Make (valid) comparisons between your book and other wildly popular works or suggest that your book will help enhance or complete a collection.

Who will help you with marketing?

Are you going to hire a publicist? Could you go on local (or national) TV or radio programs? Will the manager of your independent bookstore let you host a book signing? Can you get your friends to spread the word through social media? Does your mom's book club need a new book? With your budget in mind, start exploring your networking options. Author and motivational speaker Dr. Joey Faucette once said it perfectly: "Despite what you may think, you are not a solo driver. One day you will realize you were in the carpool lane the whole time." You'll need help getting this book to sell, so start building and cultivating important relationships now.

What

What type of book does your audience want right now?

Obviously, readers want strong, intriguing writing, but is there a theme that is popular within your genre at the moment? For example, paranormal romances are currently all the rage in young-adult fiction, and presidential biographies or exposés are popular during election years. Give the people what they want and they will be sure to buy it—and at a pretty decent price, too.

What does your book offer that others do not?

This ties in with the question above. Even if you just published the three-thousandth book on bird watching, there has to be some new and never-before-seen information in your book that can't be found anywhere else. Do a little research and highlight a handful of points that make your book unique and thus invaluable in that respect. Focus on this information when marketing your book; tell your readers that you have finally captured the albatross's mating dance or that you've even more accurately charted the migration patterns of the blue-footed booby.

What will your marketing do to draw in readers?

Are you planning to appear on local TV or radio? Do you have particularly good reviews? Will you offer a unique discount or bundling on your book when it comes out? Are you going to be at book-signing events, creating special blogs, reaching out to media across the country, or offering a package deal with another product? All of these things will be addressed in the next few chapters, but start thinking about books that have caught your eye and how they did so.

Where

Where is your audience (geographically/demographically)?

This type of analysis is important not only for your sales but also for your media interactions and press releases. If you just finished your fascinating travel guide for Los Angeles, you're probably going to want to target the L.A. area. Your customers are probably going to be located in the city and will most likely be tourists who value your expertise. Think about your book from the customer's standpoint: where and when would you want to buy the book?

Where does your audience shop?

Continuing the L.A. travel guide example, you're most likely to get buyers in gift shops, vacation-planning stores and websites, and online. They might want an e-book version for easy travel. Put yourself in your audience's shoes and figure out the top three places that readers would look for a book like yours. Then, put your book there and advertise like crazy. If the answer is less straightforward, move on to the next question.

Where are you going to sell and market your book (online, in stores, through a sales rep, with the help of a publicist, etc.)?

"All of the above" is also a great answer. The more (positive) exposure you get, the better your book will sell. We cannot stress enough the importance of having your book online, both on your own website and on Amazon, Barnes & Noble, and the iBookstore. Use your website, blog, and other social media to publicize your book among your followers, and constantly point them to where they can purchase the book online.

We discussed selling in bookstores in chapters 8 and 9, and remember that although fewer people are shopping in brick-and-mortar buildings, popular bookstores are still a great place to sell your book. It's the discovery phenomenon: readers may not have walked in looking for your book, but they will walk out with it in their shopping bag because they saw it and found it interesting.

Using a sales rep and/or a publicist can also be extremely helpful in promoting or selling your book. Find a person or company you trust and that has produced quality work and help for other authors, preferably authors with books similar to yours. The more experience the person/company has with your genre, the better. Sales reps and publicists know the inside tracks of the business and have invaluable contacts and familiarity with book sales. If it fits in your budget, hiring these pros never fails.

When

When will you start your marketing campaign?

As soon as you start writing your book. That's not to say you should send out your press release when you finish chapter 1, but you can start tweeting and posting about your upcoming book once you have a manuscript in hand. Start talking with your publisher or publicist in the early stages of book production to put together a plan for marketing. Send out your galleys or hot-off-the-press copies to book reviewers and authors so you can use their comments in your campaign.

When do you stop?

Yes, eventually you will tire of self-promotion, book promotion, and every other kind of promotion under the sun. If you don't plan on writing another book, don't want to produce a second edition, or are not getting the kind of feedback and sales that you had expected, take a break, but don't give up. Writing a book is fun, but selling a book can be real work. Don't let a few setbacks or difficulties make you forget why you wrote your book in the first place. After a year or so, if you are not having any success with your book, head back to the drawing board and try to figure out where you went wrong. Then, start from scratch with a new book or a new marketing campaign and see better results.

Why

Why is your book worth buying?

Remember chapter 2, when we talked about making your book worth the wood? If you followed this advice, you are bound to have a built-in audience. Ask an acquaintance to examine your book from a potential customer's point of view. Does your book have great plot elements? Does it contain knowledge readers could not find anywhere else? What elements does your book have that create a desire to purchase your book?

For many customers who are considering buying your book, the customer reviews posted on Amazon will help them make their decision. Check your Amazon book listing often and ask your best customers to post comments about your book. Amazon also has an "About the Author" feature that you can populate with additional information and keep your audience up to date on any other news about you and your book.

If your book is being sold in a bookstore, the packaging of your book is an important aspect to consider. By adding embossed letters, gold foil stamping, high-quality paper stock, and other premium-quality design ingredients, you can make your book stand out from your competition.

Think about how your nonfiction book will be used after the book is purchased. Does your book contain valuable information that is unique to the marketplace? Define what sets your book apart from all the other books on the same subject and focus on these benefits when you are writing the sales copy on the back of the book.

Why will your marketing approach be successful?

You have a plan. That's the bottom line. Your marketing plan will define the audience, your methods to promote the book to this audience, and your sales expectations. What can you do to visualize the success of your book?

While some authors write the book first and then develop the marketing plan, most successful nonfiction books begin with a basic marketing plan first. This way, the content is written and designed for a specific audience and takes into account how the information will be utilized.

As long as you've done your homework and are willing to put in the labor, your marketing is going to reach readers. Talk with marketing and PR professionals, with your friends in sales, and with other authors, publishers, and booksellers. Hire a pro whenever you feel out of your element. You've spent a significant amount of time and energy getting this book produced, so don't let your marketing fall by the wayside. Keep planning and plotting and changing your strategy until you find an approach that is simple and successful.

For more marketing tips, read *The Complete Guide to Book Marketing* by David Cole and *Grassroots Marketing for Authors and Publishers* by Shel Horowitz.

16

USING SOCIAL MEDIA

Beyond Facebook

Now that your website is up and running and your book has already been edited (professionally) a time or two, you're ready to start your campaign via social media. While it is possible to sell a couple thousand books without starting a Twitter account, being connected on the Internet can be an easy and relatively low-maintenance way to market your book and you, the author.

We agree that there is nothing worse than the blogger who has nothing to write about except her cats or the guy on Twitter who keeps you constantly updated on his eating and sleeping habits. But you're different; you have a book (a great book), and you have something important to say. And you're about to be a published writer, which means you can turn a phrase. Consider your social media experience one big PR venture; you always want to sound clever and interesting and remember to promote yourself to the fullest.

Jenna McCarthy, author of *The Parent Trip: From High Heels and Parties to Highchairs and Potties* and *If It Was Easy They'd Call the Whole Damn Thing the Honeymoon: Living with and Loving the TV-Addicted, Sex-Obsessed, Not-So-Handy Man You Married*, is an online guru. "I'm a social media addict," she confessed, "so that is where I started—Facebook, Twitter, my blog, and my website. You can't be afraid to say 'If you like this, please repost it to your page!' which isn't always easy, but that's what social media is all about."

In this chapter, we'll touch on a few of the most popular social media outlets, such as Facebook, Twitter, blogs, book trailers, and more. We'll skip the setup details (we're more than certain that you can create accounts on your own), but we'll give you some pointers on how to look and sound your best online and how to use your social media to generate even more book sales.

Your Website

As we discussed earlier, your website is a great place to advertise. Not only are you selling your book but also you are selling yourself. Keep your "Media" and "News/Events" pages up to date with new (and glowing) reviews, upcoming book signings, and your progress on your book trailer/screenplay/next project in the works/etc.

Also be sure that your website links to your blog, Facebook, Twitter, and any other sites you have connected to your name or your book. This rule applies in reverse for your extra social media outlets.

Facebook

Everybody is on Facebook, right? Even if you rarely check it, your friends forced you to sign up for an account to "stay in touch." Well, we have a more important assignment for you. If you are a relatively avid Facebook user on your personal page, that's great. But you should also start up a new author or book page that you can use to directly market your book so you can have fans instead of just friends.

Charles J. Orlando, author of *The Problem with Women Is Men*, has used Facebook and has gotten great results. "When I released my agent and respectfully declined a book deal with a major press, I was faced with the standard dilemma facing all authors: how to effectively promote myself and my writing. I began testing a variety of avenues: blogging, Twitter, Facebook, YouTube—but the medium that paid off was Facebook. It's really a natural fit, in that the forum lends itself to creating vertical communities and enabling interactive and engaging threaded discussion. Moreover, it was very rewarding for me personally, in that part of what was so gratifying in writing my book was the interaction I had with the participants in my research—something that was missing for me as I began promoting it. Facebook assisted me in rekindling that."

Orlando's site is ranked within the top one hundred Facebook book pages, has more than five hundred thousand fans, has led him to appear on more than forty TV and radio shows, and has helped him sell thousands and thousands of books. As of 2011, his book and Facebook page were being considered for a network television series.

How much does all of this cost? Orlando says he spends only about $100 per month on website hosting and social media apps. Not half bad, huh?

"In order for an author to be successful using social media, it has to be genuine (read: the actual person, not their 'marketing rep' or publicist)," he explains. "Moreover, what's written has to be original/unique to the medium, and it has to have a solid opinion—meaning it reflects the thoughts of the writer and doesn't concern itself with trying to please everyone. But, it's not for everyone, in that unless you have a message, you might not be able to engage and retain an interactive audience."

Impressively, Facebook doesn't even come close to consuming Orlando's life, as he is busy appearing on other shows and writing away.

"It depends on the time available," Orlando says of his involvement online. "I'm on Facebook, and I have my settings to allow all posts to my page's Wall to be put out automatically on Twitter, and I check Twitter once per day. But I'm not really active on Twitter—for me it's all Facebook. My suggestion: be on all of them (as you really need to be these days), but focus on one."

Twitter

Twitter has also taken a commanding presence in the social media world. While you are limited to a certain character count in your posts, Twitter is a great outlet for brief sound bites and updates. With every company, corporation, magazine, newspaper, movie star, and author on Twitter, it's high time you jumped on the bandwagon.

People who get the most out of Twitter are those who can dedicate a lot of time to reading, tweeting, re-tweeting, and replying to others. Twitter is often compared to a giant newsroom with headlines that are of particular interest to you, and the most successful folks on Twitter stay on top of all of that. The good news? Messages are often short, so you don't need to compose a thousand-word essay. You can "tweet" only 140 characters at a time (about the length of a text message), so the posts you read and write will be fairly brief. The downside to this is that it can be difficult to be so succinct.

Twitter is also particularly helpful for authors with personality, which is generally the case with social media apps. If you are insightful or funny or have a unique voice (and people like your book), you're going to get a ton of followers. With the short message format, your wit will need to shine through. Most authors don't have the luxury of a Justin Bieber fan craze, and you'll want to give followers a reason to read your tweets. Don't simply re-tweet or post links; get creative.

For example, "Funny or Die," which began as a comedy website for videos, photos, and comments (where users could vote on whether the content was "funny" or should "die"), has one of the most popular Twitter accounts in the world. Their tweets are hilarious and direct traffic toward their other social media sites.

Authors don't always have the luxury of being comedians, but definitely dedicate your voice to your tweets. While your followers are most likely your readers, they don't want to be constantly updated with your book sales or links to buy your latest novel. They want to know more about you and hear your opinions; tell them about your thoughts on the e-book revolution, breaking news about your book signing in Michigan, or your tips for aspiring authors. Don't tweet about what you had for dinner or that you're going to sleep or that you're going out to party (unless any of these are particularly noteworthy and relevant). Not only is it too much information but followers don't need to know your sleeping habits.

Blogs

Blogs are another great way to get your voice out on the Internet. If you don't already have a blog forum, choose one now. Blogging, like Twitter and Facebook, takes some daily dedication. Think of it as a warm-up for your books or as a channel for a genre that you don't feel you could focus on for three hundred pages. For example, if you have a good sense of humor but would be hard-pressed to write a satire, use some of that built-up wit in your blog. Readers will like to see your writing range and get a sense of your personality (which doesn't always come across in longer or published writing).

Blogs are not diaries, so resist the urge to get too personal. Besides, this particular blog is supposed to help promote your book, not air your grievances with the deli on Front Street or bash your ex. On the other hand, insight into your daily life can be entertaining. If you write a book about relationships, by all means share some of your stories and advice. Or if you created the ultimate guide to car maintenance, provide your readers with tips and photos from your own experience.

Your blog can include these appropriate personal posts, but you should certainly put some emphasis on your book writing. During the production of your book, keep a running log of all of the highs and lows, peaks and pitfalls (do not, however, trash anyone on your production team). Fans will love to see the play-by-play of the creation of your book, and other authors can learn from your triumphs and mistakes.

It's also possible to reach a wider audience if your blog is somewhat unrelated to your book. Say you've blogged for the past three years about running and have built up quite a following. Don't start from scratch, even if your new book has nothing to do with exercise. Loyal blog readers like your writing no matter the topic, and odds are they will like your book.

Book Trailers

Our personal favorite in the new technology category, book trailers are becoming all the rage.

What's a book trailer?

In essence, you create a little preview for your book. It should be under two minutes long (anything longer gives away too much) and should act just like a good movie trailer. Some authors act out scenes from the text, read especially good (but short) excerpts, or address the audience with the benefits of reading this particular book. Each genre has a budding stereotype for how to go about creating your trailer. For example, cookbooks often showcase upbeat authors or actors cooking and discussing the theme of the recipes (think along the lines of a Rachael Ray commercial). Horror novels feature creepy music, frightening or graphic photos, and powerful phrases that flash across the screen. Check out sites such as www.lightboxestrailers.com or www.bookscreening.com for current trailers.

Jenna McCarthy created a trailer to promote her book *If It Was Easy They'd Call the Whole Damn Thing the Honeymoon: Living with and Loving the TV-Addicted, Sex-Obsessed, Not-So-Handy Man You Married* (which is hilarious, by the way) and agreed to share her insights into the business.

"Until recently I was a video virgin," she admitted. "I knew that video was the 'wave of the present' and an incomparable SEO tool; I also knew that YouTube was important and that people were spending something ungodly like four hours a day on there. I was planning to do a series of what I was calling 'video shorts' that I could post on YouTube and publish to my blog and Facebook page to promote my book. I hadn't figured out how exactly I was going to pull that off when fortuitously, I met another author through my publisher. Sarah Maizes is also a humor writer and had a new trailer for her book *GOT MILF* that was hilarious. She connected me with her production team from L.A., Dan Rosen and Randy Shropshire, and I sent them my ideas. They liked them but thought it was too much. 'You need one really great video, not twenty so-so ones,' Dan, the director, told me. After seeing Sarah's trailer, I had to agree. It pretty much said it all."

What's the Point?

McCarthy put it perfectly. "I wanted my video to be something that people would pass along to their friends and ultimately [crosses fingers] go viral. The videos that achieve that illustrious and sometimes elusive status aren't necessarily the slick or overproduced ones, and they're rarely the videos that are trying hard to sell you something. Like a good movie, good trailers make people laugh (Gary Shteyngart, Dennis Cass), or they make them think/cry (Kelly Corrigan), and hopefully they make people want to buy your book." This is another route for advertising and promotion and one that you can have some fun with.

What Does It Cost?

Creating a trailer does entail a bit of a cost, a number that varies based on the quality and the type of video you produce.

"There are really no rules here yet," McCarthy said. "If you have modest acting and editing skills, you could pull off something like that for the cost of an HD Flip video camera (around $150). You can get decent music for free online, and most of us have a friend or two we could talk into 'starring' in our videos for the reasonable price of a six-pack or something similar. My video cost quite a bit relative to all of that—but I enlisted a sponsor to help cover the production and distribution costs" (more on that later).

I'm sure you're tired of hearing it, but remember that your trailer should look professional. You don't need to hire Steven Spielberg, but you also don't want to record your video with your smartphone or create it on PowerPoint. A book trailer doesn't have to break the bank, but it should promote your work and excite your readers, not turn them off with amateur acting or voiceovers for your pets.

When do I use a book trailer?

Just as your website should be up before your book, so should your book trailer. We're talking several months in advance so you can get your readers in a tizzy waiting for the release date.

"Publishers really like preorders (and the more you have, the more they are likely to print in the initial run), so I'd say sooner is better, within reason," advised McCarthy. "My book is coming out in October, and my video is going out late July. I think a little sooner would have been even better."

How do you get the word out?

Post it on YouTube! Immediately! Link to it from your website, blog, Facebook, etc. E-mail it to a few friends (or your entire address book) and ask them to forward it. Everyone wants to watch a good video, and they'll be even more excited to learn about your awesome new book.

McCarthy also recommends enlisting some professional help. "I have a publicist through Berkley, so she's helping spread the word—and I also hired a publicist to help with placing it strategically in the blogosphere. Honestly, just promoting the video could be a full-time job, so you can't get too caught up in it or you'll forget that the trailer was designed to be a sales tool for your book. The trailer costs money; the book (hopefully) makes money. That's a critical distinction you don't want to forget."

What about getting sponsored?

There are no guarantees here, and getting sponsored can be akin to finding that Ken-doll-perfect boyfriend with the convertible, mansion (with a hot tub), and impressive wardrobe. Sometimes it's just make-believe. McCarthy, however, was able to get her book sponsored by Zestra, a company that specializes in "bedroom products" (OK, arousal gels) for women—a perfect pairing for a book about dealing with an all-too-human husband.

How'd she do it? "I made a phone call. Literally—it was very spontaneous. I hadn't really decided how much money I was going to spend on marketing my book or how exactly I was going to market it, but I knew that I wasn't going to do a lot of sitting around in dusty bookstores signing books being bought by friends who would have bought them anyway. I thought the video idea was fun and different and also—and this is critical—would make my publisher happy.

"When I found out how much the video was going to cost and how much updating my website was going to cost and factored in the time/resources it would take to get it out into the world, a lightbulb went off: I needed a sponsor! I thought, 'Who do I know who might be interested in reaching the same audience I am that might want to be part of this (and also might have some cash to fork over)?' One company sprang to mind immediately, so I just picked up the phone and called. I had worked with them several times and knew and liked the CEO tremendously. When I got her on the phone, I basically blurted, 'I have a new book coming out, and I am making an awesome video to promote it, and I'm looking for someone to help underwrite the cost in exchange for some cross promotion, and I haven't really thought out all of the details, but would you be interested in seeing a written proposal?' She said, 'Sure!' and I sat down and wrote up a one-page proposal. She made one tiny change, signed it, and I had a check within a week. Not only did I have someone sharing the bulk of the cost with me, but they have their own customers and their own mailing lists and aren't just willing but excited to promote me and the book and video as well. It's a triple win."

YouTube

Book trailers lead us nicely into this topic. Post any book-related video you have to YouTube: interviews, book trailers, promotional pieces—anything you have that will help amp up the hype. As McCarthy said, YouTube is a very high-traffic search engine and can be a great tool. The moment you have some usable book footage, create an account and start uploading. Include specific tags and titles (e.g., "Jane Doe's *First Book*") so your readers can have easy access to your videos.

Using Google Analytics

Google is making the Internet better and better every day. Google Analytics and Google AdWords are two of the best products out there for online marketing. Google also offers tons of other products, programs, and seminars to make you more effective on the web, so visit www.google.com and search for programs that suit your needs.

Go to www.google.com/analytics to learn about the analytics program, which helps you determine who is looking at your website and what kind of information viewers want.

According to the site, Google Analytics is "the enterprise-class web analytics solution that gives you rich insights into your website traffic and marketing effectiveness. Powerful, flexible and easy-to-use features now let you see and analyze your traffic data in an entirely new way. With Google Analytics, you're more prepared to write better-targeted ads, strengthen your marketing initiatives and create higher converting websites." Sound intriguing? It's better than that: Google Analytics will change your life (online at least). You get numbers, charts, percentages, pie charts, maps—in short, every organizational tool that you've ever dreamed of—to help you optimize your success. You can see how many people visit your site, how much time they spend browsing around, how they got to your page, and more.

Big-name companies and organizations such as RE/MAX, the American Cancer Society, and Costco swear by Google Analytics, so why shouldn't you? We suggest also looking into Google AdWords, which is a great way to help you advertise. Using AdWords puts your ad up on Google search pages when someone types in your keywords. Check out adwords.google.com for details.

To Wrap Up ...

By the time this book hits the shelves, it's quite likely a new social media app will have popped up. Try your best to stay on top of what is popular (you don't need to sign up for every beta release you see) and market your book accordingly.

> *"The person who gets the most rejection letters will, in the end, get the most acceptance phone calls. She's put herself out there. She's learning from the editorial responses. She's writing away. She's believing in herself."*
>
> —GAIL CARSON LEVINE

BOOK REVIEWS

The Good, the Bad, the Paid For

OK, so you are ready for the cold, hard truth. You are ready, right? If you are sending your book (or, better yet, if you've been planning well and are ahead of that stage, the galley of your book) off to be reviewed, that is what you are saying to yourself and the world of book critics. Don't just think that you are sending your book off to a faceless nitpicker, though. It will be a real person who opens your package, even if it's just the newest intern in the mailroom. Eventually, your book will make its way to a living, breathing human being. Who is that? Who is your ideal book reviewer? When you package up your book, your press release, a list of endorsements, and a cover letter, who do you imagine will be evaluating your package?

Someone in a good mood, for starters! Someone unaffected and unimpressed by names such as Random House, Knopf, and Farrar, Strauss and Giroux. Someone smart and kind. A lover of ideas, new writers, old wisdom, fresh starts, and preserved tradition. Someone who didn't leave home after an argument, didn't face gridlock, and didn't get caught in the rain. Of course, none of these things are in your control, but you can hope, can't you? You can hope for someone with the sensibilities of Lynne Sharon Schwartz.

"I like to think of a new book as a mysterious geological treasure, a rock never before handled," she wrote in an article titled "Getting Started in Book Reviewing" and published in the magazine *The Writer*. "The delighted discoverers' first, most natural response is, what have we here? I hold the rock in the palm of my hand to examine it. What are its colors, its contours, its special beauty (or ugliness)? Is it like others I've seen, enough like them, even to fit into a generic category? Is it more or less beautiful than those of its kind? Or is it, though it bears a surface family resemblance, distinguished by intriguing, individual markings?"

Janice Harayda, former book editor of the *Cleveland Plain Dealer*, puts it this way: "As a reviewer, I've always tried to ask: what did this author set out to do, and how well did he or she do it? Instead of, 'What do I think this author ought to have set out to do?'"

Sounds reasonable, right? The most important characteristic of your ideal critic should be that he or she is read by others—and read not only by others but also by those whose opinions matter and matter so much that they influence behavior. That means that they inspire their readers to buy your book—and that is the real power of a book reviewer. Their words inspire action. Whether that action is to make a reader buy your book, to make a librarian shelve your book, or to make a bookseller stock your book, good book reviewers function in the real world of publishing and not off in a bunker somewhere. Maybe their action is to inspire writers and publishers to produce better books, but that is still action.

Forget the naysayer who says that critics don't matter, especially to independent publishers. Reviews do sell books. Think about it. Haven't you bought a book after reading a review of it?

"It doesn't even matter if the book was given a thumbs-up or thumbs-down," says mystery writer JA Konrath. "I read reviews for content, not opinion, and reviews alert me to the existence of the types of books I normally buy. If this works on me, I'm guessing it works on other people."

So, if book reviewers function in the real world, their work is a part of it and influenced by it. They may not like that idea much, thinking that they set public opinion rather than being manipulated by it, but they'd be wrong. Critics are human, and humans are all affected by popular opinion. "Well," you sniff, "my book is such high-brow literature that no critic worth his or her salt would dare pass it up." If your book can be compared favorably to works such as Michael Cunningham's *The Hours* or Khaled Hosseini's T*he Kite Runner*, J. K. Rowling's *Harry Potter* series or the work of Philip Pullman, Stephen R. Covey's business philosophy books or Suze Orman's money management books, then you may be right. If, however, you don't have Hosseini's delicate phrasing or cultural background, Pullman's limitless imagination, Rowling's vision, Covey's spark, or Orman's platform, you're going to have to come up with other ways to entice reviewers.

There is always some genre of book that is in fashion at any particular time, and if that's the genre in which you're writing and publishing, your chances of having your book reviewed in trade and consumer publications are good. Very good, in fact. If that's not the case, you're going to have to get creative and maybe even be satisfied with print inches in niche journals and regional publications. Review space is shrinking, just as the number of books being published every year is skyrocketing. As a matter of fact, that shrinking space alone is one of the biggest pressures on review space.

Newspapers, once filled with pages and pages of book review space, are cutting back. Hacking back, even. The situation has become so dire that the National Book Critics Circle (NBCC) began a campaign to "save" the book review.

"Book coverage has been cut back or slashed all together, moved, winnowed, filled with more wire copy, or generally been treated as expendable," the group states on its website. "And we're getting tired of it. We're tired of watching individual voices from local communities passed over for wire copy. We're tired of book editors with decades of experience shown the exit. We're tired of shrinking reviews. We're tired of hearing newspapers fret and worry over the future of print while they dismantle the section of the paper which deals most closely with the two things which have kept them alive since the dawn of printing presses: the public's hunger for knowledge and the written word."

Still, NBCC may indeed be telling it like it is, but what can an independent publisher do about it? A lot. First, if you're at a book event and the petition being circulated by the NBCC is passed to you, sign it. You'll be in good company. Writers James Lee Burke, Michael Connelly, Karin Slaughter, Denis Lehane, Allan Gurganus, Anne Fadiman, Gary Shteyngart, Todd Gitlin, Robert Draper, Craig Nova, Clyde Edgerton, Julie Phillips, Troy Jollimore, and dozens of others have signed it, too. Second, write a letter to your local newspaper, whether that's a major one such as the *Atlanta Journal-Constitution* or something more hometown such as the *Leelanau Enterprise*. Tell them that you want a healthy book section and that you read the paper partly because of it. The book review has an important purpose in society.

"We are the pilot fish, those strange, tiny creatures, which go in front of the real thing, the great shark or the great whale, warning, saying to people, 'It's coming,'" wrote George Steiner in *The Writer's Chapbook* by George Plimpton. "A good teacher, a good critic says, 'This is the real thing. Here's why. Please read it, read it, come on and buy it. Go and get it.'"

Of course, authors whose previous books have been best sellers get preferential treatment. So, the best way to get reviewed is to be a best-selling writer, because then reviewers will seek you out. Daunting but true. The next best way is to write/publish an "important" book on an "important" topic, such as war, archaic history, dead writers, and Third World countries. Not best sellers but important work, nonetheless. Last, review space goes to the new authors, midlist books, and independent and self-publishers. That's you, probably.

Signing a petition feels good, and so does writing a letter to the editor, but will it help you get reviewed and sell books? Probably not. At least, not for a long while, if ever. And, consider that some publications even have a policy against reviewing any title from a self-publisher. Listen to the words of critic Bob Hoover of the *Pittsburgh Post-Gazette*, who explains why he won't review self-published books:

> "Not all books are created equally. Some are bought by commercial publishers who believe that the work is good enough to be appreciated by readers, to carry the publisher's name and to earn both the writers and publisher money."

> To ensure the book's quality, publishers subject it to professional editing and fact-checking, including plagiarism and legal issues. Experienced editors also work with writers to polish their work, frequently demanding rewriting and occasionally recasting of characters and plot.

> "By the time a trade book is ready for publication, it is a finished product backed by publishers who have staked their reputation on that book. Other writers chose to pay a printing operation to produce copies of their work, a process that has grown more sophisticated thanks to the print-on-demand services of Internet-based companies.

> "Because these books do not go through the rigorous examination, editing, and guarantees of a trade publisher, the *Post-Gazette* chooses not to review them. Without that initial work and backing, self-published books hold the possibility of exposing the newspaper to libel and plagiarism charges.

"Due to the large amount of books sent to the newspaper yearly, the policy on self-published books also works to narrow the candidates for review."

OK, take a deep breath. As an independent publisher, you may disagree with each and every word in Bob Hoover's review policy, but it's important to know what you're up against when seeking print reviews in established publications with a large readership. For each review copy that you send out, learn the review policy and decide whether your chance of being reviewed is great enough to warrant sending in a copy of your book, a press release, and a cover letter. If yes, follow the review policy to the letter. If not, move on.

Once you've sent your book out for review, sit back and wait and get ready now to handle a bad review or two. If your book is timely, well produced, and clearly written and if you're really working smart and hard, you're going to get reviewed and sometimes maybe even badly. As tempting as it may be, don't despair. Listen to J.A. Konrath and your own good sense. Reviews bring attention to a book, even if they're critical or not as glowing as you'd like. Being ignored is far worse than a bad review. "Critics are like woodpeckers," said the poet Henry Wadsworth Longfellow, "who, instead of enjoying the fruit and shadow of a tree, hop incessantly around the trunk pecking holes in the bark to discover some little worm or other." Sometimes, critics just like to spew. That's why they're critics, many of them. If you receive a bad review, settle down and read it again in a few hours or a few days and try to determine whether it's objective or just mean. "I have long felt that any reviewer who expresses rage and loathing for a novel is preposterous. He or she is like a person who has put on full armor and attacked a hot fudge sundae or banana split," said Kurt Vonnegut.

Sure, maybe a reviewer looked at your book's worm through a magnifying glass and showed it to others, too. Maybe he or she attacked your hot fudge sundae. Well, now you know where

> *If your book is timely, well produced, and clearly written ... you're going to get reviewed ...*

to improve. Your job is just to "enjoy the fruit and shadow of a tree" and show all of your good points to readers, in whatever manner you can think of.

Here are some places that might be interested in reviewing your book. We cannot stress enough the importance of following each publication's guidelines down to the most trivial point. Jim Barnes, editor of *Independent Publisher*, estimates that 60 percent or more of the books not selected for review are weeded out because they do not follow the magazine's review submission guidelines.

- BookReview.com
- *ForeWord's* Clarion Reviews
- *Independent Publisher Magazine*
- Kirkus Discoveries
- National Book Critics Circle
- *The New York Review of Books*
- PW Select
- *San Francisco Book Review*
- *The Washington Independent Review of Books*

Below are some basic submission guidelines, but be sure to visit the website of the reviewer or make a phone call to be sure you're covering all your bases.

- Include a short and sweet cover letter. Introduce yourself, briefly discuss why you think your book should be considered for review, and shoot a little praise toward the reviewer and the publication for good measure.
- Submit a copy of a bound galley, finished book, e-book, or audiobook. Most review magazines do not accept unbound galleys or periodicals.
- Send your book prior to publication date or less than ninety days after the pub date.

- Include a cover sheet with the following information: title, author, publisher, address, phone number, website, page count, cover style, price, ISBN number, and publication month and year.
- Send a follow-up e-mail to the reviewer to confirm receipt of your title, thanking him or her for considering your book.
- If you're entering your book online, be sure to include a cover scan and book synopsis (150–250 words) to make it easier to complete your listing.
- Don't overdo it on the press kit. Reviewers are likely to throw out (or at least not read) giant packets of author info or unusable merchandise such as posters or obnoxious figurines.
- Do send nicely done and related materials if the additional items look professional and add to your book. For example, some children's books come with a stuffed animal. Some publishers and authors send their catalog with a submission.
- Send food and/or a couple of twenties along with your book. Reviewers can always use a snack or some pocket money. (We're only kidding. About sending food and money, that is …).

18

Advertising and Special Sales

Selling Direct to Consumer

What are special sales? Any sale you make that doesn't involve a bookstore. There are many publishers who have made a small fortune in selling directly to consumers in tightly defined markets. The ways are varied: advertising in trade magazines, direct mail, sales through seminars, and simply doing a host of media interviews and giving out an 800 number to listeners. Although it will challenge all of your entrepreneurial skills, direct selling is a great way to sell books. From learning the mechanics and logistics of the various direct sale channels, to making pitches with near-surgical precision to the target audience, to creating a pitch that's heard above all the others, you'll have to do the work, but the payoff will be worth it. Each book you sell will capture the full retail price with very few returns.

Besides hard work, selling direct takes creativity and capital. But those who succeed think of their work as the ultimate in entrepreneurship and wouldn't do business any other way.

Advertising in Trade Magazines

Most publishers already know what kind of magazines their customers read through experience, research, and intuition. Still, it pays to do some definitive research before placing an ad for your book in a magazine.

Go to the library or go online and find *Consumer Magazine, Agri-Media Rates and Data*, and *Audit Bureau of Circulations*. There you'll find everything you need to know about a magazine publication: rates, editorial focus, and circulation numbers. Audited circulation means the actual number of subscribers. Circulation means estimated number of readers, including the recipient plus family and friends. If you've written a book for business professionals, check out the reference book *Business Publication Rates and Data*. Order a sample copy of each of the magazines you're considering and examine the classified and display ads to determine whether your advertisement belongs alongside.

For the most cost-effective advertising, place your ads in the most tightly niched magazine possible. Many publishers can't afford to pay full price for a magazine display ad (it wouldn't pay off in sales) and are able to negotiate a 50 percent discount. Ed Hinkelman of World Trade Press, a publishing firm, said he always asks for a discount—and gets it. "We wouldn't be in business today if we had to pay full price," he said.

To get the best results for your ad:

1. Offer more than one item: Cynthia Kim, publisher of martial arts books, said advertisements in niche or trade magazines can be extremely effective, but it's necessary to advertise more than one book in order to make a profit. An ad that offers $40 worth of books/videos pays back the ad investment much quicker than an ad offering a $10 book, for example.

    Besides bundling books, she suggests offering an incentive, such as, "Order three martial arts books and receive a free sixty-minute videotape."

If calls are coming to you directly, offer buyers a related book that you've published at X amount of dollars off. They get a bargain, and you've made a sale—plus you save on postage, mailing supplies, and handling.

2. Start small: Test out your copy in a small classified ad before jumping to bigger and/or more frequent ads. Headlines make the real difference. Try three or four different ones. To track the ad's success, put a code number in the address to be used when ordering. "SA01XX," for example, could mean *Sports Afield*, January of 20XX.

3. Write short copy and write it convincingly. State the benefit to the reader clearly, genuinely, enticingly, and without hyperbole. Use warmth; don't sound like you're selling snake oil.

   Some publishers make the fatal error of bragging about the author and/or company in the headline. Self-promotion does not sell books.

Getting on TV or on the Radio

Before spending a dollar for paid advertising, figure out how to get a story about your book into newspapers or magazines or schedule an interview on radio or television for free. The objective, of course, is to get the listener or reader interested in your book and eager to order via a toll-free number (try to choose a number that's easy to remember).

When pitching a story, think of yourself as an expert talking on a specific angle related to your book: Are schools dumbing down the curriculum? How to outmaneuver the IRS before tax day. Ten simple things you can do to become a happier parent. Has gymnastics robbed young girls of healthy bones? Ten no-cost or low-cost ideas for a romantic Valentine's Day.

To get a busy producer's attention, mail, e-mail, or fax a story idea and follow up with a phone call.

If your pitch relates to today's front-page news, definitely fax your story idea. The best scenario would be to be picked up by the newswire services, which file a single article that runs concurrently in newspapers and online venues across the country.

Prepare well for the interview. Anticipate the questions they'll ask. Tease the listener with the benefits of the book by discretely mentioning specific chapters and exactly how the information can benefit the reader. Have a joke or two ready. Tell the audience how to get your book and that if they call today, they'll get something special such as an autographed book, a special report, free shipping, a box of Valentine candy, or a $5 discount. But give them an incentive to order immediately.

Public Speaking

Are you a good public speaker? Are you funny? Have you published a book in a sought-after area of expertise? If so, consider giving professional seminars. It's a great way to attract the right kind of customers for your book. A lot of authors find that they can draw in customers with a low-cost, or even free, seminar and then sell books, videos, or audiotapes afterward in what are called back-of-the-room sales. Others have grown an entire career around their book, using it as an anchor of credibility, and conduct seminars year-round.

How can you get into the business of speaking for money? The avenues are varied and can lead to different destinations. Some speakers specialize in what are called public seminars, in which the public at large is invited to a public gathering place, such as a hotel. Others hire themselves out for in-house seminars, in which a corporation, church, or nonprofit association fills the seats and pays the speaker a preestablished fee.

If you give public seminars, very specifically target your audience. For example, focus not on motorcycle owners but on Harley-Davidson owners who are having trouble with their Cafe Racer models from 1984 to 1995.

There's another decision to be made when considering how to go about becoming a paid speaker. Should you use an agent? Some people use what are called speaker bureaus, which act as agents. A bureau essentially finds work for the speaker and takes care of any and all details regarding the engagement. All the speaker has to do is show up. The bureau generally takes half the speaking fee in return.

A speaker's bureau, however, isn't for everybody. A maxim in the industry: When you need an agent, he or she doesn't need you. When you no longer need an agent, he or she would love to put you on the roster. That's not always true, however. Particularly sexy subjects in a well-delivered speech will grab the attention of an agent. One woman, for example, is giving speeches around the country about her experience posing for Playboy magazine.

Another avenue is to find an organization to cosponsor a seminar, such as a church, chamber of commerce, or Rotary Club. This gives you credibility and helps solve the biggest dilemma of giving a seminar: filling seats. For example, if your book focuses on a Christian approach to money management, you could ask churches to cosponsor a seminar on the subject. You deliver the seminar; they publicize it to their congregation. That begs the question: what percentage of the receipts do you share with the church? If it handles all the details and all you have to do is show up to make the presentation, then you might give it two-thirds of the receipts. If you do all the work (letter writing, sign-ups, registration, making handout copies, room planning, refreshments), then take 90 percent.

Going into the seminar business usually requires a very serious investment of time and money. But some people have slipped selling books into their existing lifestyle. Michelle Beaudry, a touring stand-up comedian for more than two decades, sells nearly all of her comedy books at her shows. The money from these sales paid for all her publishing expenses and was still better than selling through distributors, as there were no expenses incurred in shipping or returns.

Here's her advice on pitching a book without offending your crowd: overselling the availability of titles while on stage is the kiss of death. If your act reads like an infomercial, people get annoyed. They have paid a cover charge, after all. So consider yourself warned: direct sales have to be handled delicately.

Here are some tips to get you started:

- Do you feel you could use a little education in the humor department? *Read Comedy Writing Secrets* by Mel Heiltzer.
- Before going professional, join Toastmasters to sharpen your speaking skills. It's a nationwide public-speaking organization, and there is probably a group that meets near you. "Twelve years ago I was mainly mute in front of four or five people," said Alex Moore, former book review editor at an independent review journal. "It was embarrassing. 'Try Toastmasters,' a humanitarian said. I did. I learned to control nervousness, organize my presentations, use eye contact and gestures, voice and pacing variations. I'm now undaunted when appearing in front of 100 publishers at Book Expo America."
- Also, volunteer to speak for free at local service clubs. Videotape your speech; it's your product, and people will want to see it before booking you.
- Try giving speeches for free and request that the audience fill out forms afterward. Ask them to suggest future seminar topics. If you detect a trend, seize it. Develop a new speech and market it; use the addresses from the questionnaires as a mailing list.
- Excerpt the positive things people say about you on the questionnaire for your promotional brochure. (Of course, make sure the person indicates on the questionnaire that it's OK to quote).

- Offer an upsell. For example, if you give a three-hour seminar, the upsell is a two-day workshop.
- At the end of your presentation, walk to the back of the room while your introducer announces you'll be signing books. Ask for a volunteer if you need one, and be prepared to accept credit cards.
- Read Paul Karasik's book, *How to Make It Big in the Seminar Business*, published by McGraw-Hill. It's chock-full of advice and resources (including 160 public seminar companies and 543 of the best seminar sites). He offers detailed advice for those interested in conducting seminars.

Selling via Infomercials

Does your book deliver a huge promise to the masses? Can it solve a chronic problem that's deeply, even painfully, felt by most Americans? Will they become richer, skinnier, or more youthful looking by faithfully following the instructions in your book? Can your book show them how to finally buy a house with zero down? Does your new book promise good-tasting meals in fewer than thirty minutes? Will people find money and happiness in their lives by studying your book, *The Top Ten Behavioral Traits of Successful People?*

Does this sound like an infomercial? It should, because these are exactly the kinds of books that do very well in long commercial formats.

Infomercials are largely the province of exercise equipment and household items that are designed to make life more convenient. Well-made infomercials cost anywhere from $50,000 to $500,000 to produce and air on national television.

Yet it is possible to produce infomercials as cheaply as $1,000 for fifteen minutes and air them on a tiny cable channel for $85. Will it work for your book? Good question. It's extremely rare to see a book advertised in an infomercial. If you are considering this medium, it's imperative to call other advertisers on the target channel to see what results they've received.

Before you invest any money in an infomercial, take note of Peter Bieler's key criteria listed in his book *This Business Has Legs:*

- Is your product right for direct response? Does it demonstrate well? If it's a service, is it going to have repeat business?
- If you go with long form, what format do you choose? Some formats include a newsmagazine dominated by location reports, a talk show with a host and guests, a "storymercial" with a story line and characters, a demonstration show, or a seminar with a speaker and an audience.
- Does your copy strategy work? What compelling promise can you make about using the product that will make people want to buy it? Don't leave this to your copywriter. You know the product better than anyone.
- Are you casting the right spokesperson? Celebrity or noncelebrity, male or female, young or old, the wrong spokesperson is worse than none at all.
- Is your offer effective? Have you looked closely at your payment plan, guarantee, price point, and premiums?

Infomercials work well only for books that are very clear in their benefits. Because this format is so expensive, it's wise to offer a collection of related books. Before investing any money, tread lightly. Marketing maniac Dan Kennedy once said that only one in sixteen infomercials makes any money.

ADVERTISING ON HOME-SHOPPING CHANNELS

On September 24, 1994, 155,000 copies of *In the Kitchen with Bob* were sold to QVC watchers. Think of it. Never before in history were so many copies of one book sold in a single day. A year later, 1,495 sets of books on how to win at casinos were sold within several minutes.

About 158 million people tune into home-shopping channels every day of the week, making it a challenge for these TV retailers to fill up hours and hours of programming. This has made the major TV retailers hungry for new, unique, and unseen products. So what small publishers consider a liability—their inability to get books into general bookstores and in the mainstream media—is, in fact, an asset for home-shopping television. These very same books will seem brand new and special to the viewing audience.

"We're constantly looking for new products to feed this machine because we've got to reinvent it every day," said Home Shopping Network Vice President John Pinocci in the newsletter *Nation's Business*. "That leaves us open too, and motivated to having small vendors and manufacturers present goods to us."

How many books can you sell with one appearance on a home-shopping channel? The luckiest publishers have reaped more than a million dollars with a single appearance on QVC, although on average about three thousand books are sold. That's still terrific, considering it sometimes takes two to three years and heavy promotion dollars to sell that many.

What sorts of books do well? The book's topic has to be timely or fit in with one of the TV retailer's upcoming themes. Like an infomercial, the book should be able to solve a deeply felt, chronic problem, which could be something as simple as facing the prospect of cooking dinner every night. Authoritative books on child rearing, however, don't do well. Those with demonstration possibilities do best. As always, make the lead catchy; focus on the rewards the readers will reap from your book as opposed to the simple fact that it was published.

In general, publishers can expect a 50 percent discount with freight paid, with the right for the TV retailer to return any unsold books. Returns average about 7 to 9 percent, well below the book industry average. If the TV retailer is confident that viewers won't return the book, it may offer a 55 percent discount with guaranteed no returns.

If a publisher has good business judgment, direct marketing can be one of the most satisfying aspects of selling a book. Your success is dependent on your business savvy as opposed to market forces beyond your control. Likewise, you control your expenses. Just keep in mind that before investing a substantial amount of money in this channel, it is imperative to conduct small market tests to gauge your ultimate success.

19

BOOK AWARDS AND BOOK CLUBS

Shiny Stickers, Exposure, and Prestige

BOOK AWARDS

It's amazing what a little sticker can do for a book. Your eye is drawn to it, you pick up the book with renewed interest, you put it on the counter (or in your online shopping cart), and you buy that book. Why? Because a sticker (ahem, an award) means that someone important liked this book. We read book reviews for the same reason; awards generally come from credible people or institutions and can provide us with a quick and easy way to judge what's between the covers.

WHY ENTER?

Because awards sell books! Why do the Oscars exist? Because awards sell movie tickets! Why does the town sheriff wear a shiny star? To show that he or she is important! Publishing great books is difficult, important work, and you deserve a shiny star in recognition of that work.

Entering your titles in awards programs can take time, money, and effort, but the possible payoffs include financial reward, personal satisfaction, and prestige. Awards are a great morale boost for all those involved, and they influence reviewers and buyers. A book award is an excellent PR tool, and since most award shows don't charge you too much, it's probably one of the least expensive routes to promoting your book.

The cons? You may not win. But even this has a silver lining (if you like constructive criticism, that is). Consider losing a test, a test for yourself and your writing. Look at the books that were winners in your category and try to figure out what made them better. If you can't find a single thing, you're not looking hard enough. Be objective with your work (which is always difficult) and use what you learn to better your next book.

How are books judged?

Book awards judges are very good at assessing a book's quality, much as a buyer at a bookstore or library determines whether to purchase. The further a book makes it into the judging process, especially in fiction categories, the more likely it will be read completely and by multiple people. Even if you don't win, it's likely that your book has gotten some new eyes, some new recommendations, and possibly some reviews.

Which awards should I enter?

It all depends on your budget and your book. Search for your genre's book awards (e.g., "children's book awards") online and skim through the listings. Many awards require membership with the host company or service, and others are open only to specific books or authors. Look for one or two awards that seem like a good fit for you and have a reasonable entry fee. Also, awards with multiple categories offer more opportunities to win and a better fit for your book.

Book Clubs

Some book club deals provide a pile of easy cash to a publisher, while other book club deals are no deals at all. You have to carefully analyze each offer before signing on. In many cases the monetary reward is marginal, yet it is important to consider some of the other advantages of signing up with a book club. First and foremost, publishers can capitalize on the prestige of getting their books accepted into a club, particularly if chosen by a major club such as Book-of-the-Month Club or Literary Guild or one of their specialty clubs.

Publishers often tout this when pitching their book to libraries, distributors, foreign publishers, etc.

"The money is not that great," agreed book marketing consultant Kate Bandos. "You shouldn't expect to make much or any money. You're doing it for the exposure and the status. Even with lesser-known clubs, people are always hesitant to stick their neck out and say, 'This is a great book.' If someone else has supposedly looked through thousands of cookbooks or the *How to Make a Sweater Book* and picked this one, it's a stamp of approval. It's already been taken out of the slush pile and put in the spotlight."

Another plus to signing up with a book club is that a book club order can potentially reduce your overall printing costs. If the club piggybacks its order onto your print run, the increased quantity can reduce the printing bill by approximately 10 percent.

Third, you don't have to worry about returns. A book club keeps all the books it buys.

The club is buying a subsidiary right: the right to produce and publish the books itself (sometimes it buys the books directly from your inventory at cost, which saves the club the trouble of printing books itself).

A final positive: book clubs reach buyers you may not be able to reach otherwise. By advertising your book through a book club, you are increasing the universe of your book sales.

A small publisher's book usually finds interest in the smaller or specialized clubs of the majors. Check out LiteraryMarketPlace.com to see a full listing of clubs and ask around among your colleagues for advice. The key to marketing your book to a club is finding the specific club whose audience matches the targeted audience of your book.

A book club is typically defined as offering members a selection or selections each month, fully described in a brochure. If the member fails to send back a response card stating that no book or another book is desired, the selection is automatically shipped. (Some catalogs call themselves a book club when, in fact, they are simply offering books for purchase.) With BOMC's Smart Reader Rewards program, members don't have to return a card but can order their selections by phone or visit the program's website, www.smartreaderrewards.com.

The typical book club will offer royalties of up to 10 percent based on the club's retail price, generally 70 to 80 percent of the book's original price. When a book club buys rights to a book, it can offer the book however it chooses, including offering it as a premium (books offered as an incentive to get someone to join or as a reward for heavy book orders: "Buy four books and get one free").

Royalties on premium books are very low, at about 4 percent. Generally, the author and publisher split all royalty money. Each book club deal is different, although essentially the book club pays the publisher for the right to offer a book to its members for a specific time, usually two to five years. Some clubs will manufacture their own books and pay royalties. Some will piggyback onto the publisher's print run, paying $X a book plus royalties. Some book clubs purchase books outright from the publisher's existing stock. Because book clubs often pay a standard dollar amount for books (which they assume is cost), book deal profits often depend on how savvy the publisher is at getting a low manufacturing cost, Bandos said.

What should you expect as an advance? Typically, book clubs pay half of what they expect to earn based on their first order. Advances for a book purchased by a major club can reach as high as $100,000 and even more but far less for unpredictable sellers (in the hundreds of dollars versus thousands of dollars).

One more note: book club purchases are nonreturnable; however, some contracts will include a clause that gives the book club the right to remainder books if the publisher doesn't want to buy them back at the original cost. The potential danger, of course, is that the club may flood the market with cheap remaindered books at a time when you're trying to sell them at full price. These contracts are negotiable; try to get this clause stricken.

How to get your book considered

Large book clubs like to see your book while it's still in manuscript form, six to nine months in advance of publication. Smaller book clubs prefer galleys but are willing to consider books even after they're published.

Cover letters to a book club's acquisition editor should reflect that you clearly understand the club members' preference for books. Mention titles that are similar to yours that have proven popular in the club. If the club has never listed a similar title, give some good reasons why your title would indeed appeal to its members. You'll also need to include the estimated publication date, estimated number of pages, a brief description of the book and summary of its content, and the number and type of illustrations. Also very helpful are photocopies of sample illustrations and brief biographical material about the author, noting any previous books.

Add force to the letter by mentioning plans for a media tour or the fact that the author has been mentored by a famous author who is going to put his or her weight behind the book or that the U.S. surgeon general wrote a testimonial on the back cover.

"You can send us a galley and then send us a finished book with reviews, and that's fine," said Judy Estrine, acquisition editor for the former Doubleday Book Club. "It helps if we see something more than once. It's what the big houses do. They send us an advanced galley, then an uncorrected copy, then the finished book. These things establish a relationship. Don't give up and get depressed. It's really the name of the game to be in our face."

Follow up your first query with news to encourage acceptance of the book, for example, the book has gone into a second printing, quotes from advance book reviews, news of an audio rights or movie rights sale, etc. In the case of books chosen as a major selection or alternate selection, the book clubs often go into a bidding war of sorts.

Although the larger book clubs prefer to see manuscripts, they will buy books after they're published, particularly the specialized clubs. Jane Perkins, editorial assistant for Quality Paperback Books, said she combs small-press catalogs for books.

"I like unique, interesting, vampire-type stuff, especially humor," she said. "If I think it's going to be big, normally I want the book. It's always helpful to get promotional literature, but reviews are best, awards they've won, and sales reports. I want to know if it's gone into a second printing."

Go online to find a full listing of book clubs throughout the country (and world). Start out with one or two and see how successful your book can be.

20

CATALOG SALES

Big Advantages over Retail Sales

Most publishers originally decide to pursue catalog sales not only to tap into a new market but also to sell books without the bookstore-type headaches of heavy returns and long, drawn-out payments.

Catalog sales offer big advantages over retail sales. Most catalogs pay within thirty days of receiving your invoice and almost always buy on a nonreturnable basis. Another benefit is that independent publishers have just as much chance of breaking into the catalog market as do the New York publishing firms.

Most publishers discover that there are a couple of fallout benefits. First, a book receives wonderful exposure in catalogs, particularly prestigious catalogs such as that of Crate and Barrel. That exposure can lead to additional sales in other outlets, such as gift store or bookstore chains, according to John Storey, founder of Storey Publishing in North Adams, Massachusetts.

"When Crate and Barrel picks you up, it gives the book unbelievable publicity," he said. "It's like a rising tide that other outlets want to get on."

Second, catalog sales allow you to glean valuable marketing data for free. If a particular book does well in a catalog, you can learn exactly what kind of people will buy your book.

Conversely, if it does poorly, you'll know what kind of people won't buy your book.

"Basically, the catalog will tell you precisely the audience that it mails to and help you pinpoint your own audience," Storey said. "This information is just as important as the sales you'll get."

So how do you get your book onto the pages of a catalog? Your strategy will require a mix of marketing savvy and hard work. The two keys are extensive research at the front end and highly persuasive and persistent query letters.

Success Stories

Getting into the right catalog at the right time can translate into thousands of book sales, even for a book that you might consider a has-been. If a catalog does well with your book, it will probably keep placing orders year after year.

John Storey tells of the title *Let It Rot*, a book on backyard composting first published in 1975 with satisfactory sales of about thirty-five thousand.

"The book did well, but back then it appealed mostly to the hardcore country crowd," Storey said. "Since then, landfills have closed and the people in Birmingham, Michigan, don't know what to do with their grass clippings. The book wasn't doing much—selling about 50 a month—so we pitched it to Plow and Hearth and Garden Supply Co. We've sold more than 250,000 copies since then and printed three editions. It gained a whole new life."

To convince the two catalogs that composting was indeed a new trend among suburbanites, Storey enclosed a *New York Times Sunday Magazine* feature on composting.

In one unusual success story, a catalog was responsible for the creation of a book. Sounds True is a mail-order company that specializes in personal and spiritual development audiotapes. One of its early audiotapes was recorded by Claris Pinkola Estes. After the tape came out, a publisher asked Estes to write her ideas in book form. The result? The best-selling *Women Who Run with the Wolves*.

Here's an example of how a creative entrepreneur used catalogs to achieve her dual mission of selling books and encouraging girls to read. Pleasant T. Rowland founded her own mail-order company, Pleasant Company, to sell the American Girls collection of books, dolls, and accessories. Each historically accurate doll comes with a book that traces the life of a nine-year-old heroine. Each one of the books depicts a different era in American history. The books end with a nonfiction account of what life was really like.

Mrs. Rowland believes that direct marketing has been the best way to achieve her goal of fostering a love for reading while saving money on mass media advertising.

Taking Aim at Your Market

The first things every publisher must do are study catalogs and determine which ones best fit a specific book. There are catalogs specializing in honey, aquariums, cats, supplies for nurses, weird scientific inventions, ethnic crafts, and time-saving books especially for women. There's even a catalog for single women that offers eligible bachelors!

Catalogs take specialization to the ultimate degree. That means you need to figure out exactly what kind of people would buy your book. Draw up a profile: How much money do they earn, what is their lifestyle, what are their interests? Where do they live? What kind of catalogs do they favor? Say your book is on financial scholarships for nontraditional students. Your job is to find a catalog for older adults who are seeking a career change, live in a college town, and have made a mail-order purchase in the past six months.

When choosing a catalog, look for not only a product fit but also an image fit: Does it use color? One-color catalogs can look chintzy. Other criteria include the following: Does the catalog have a toll-free number, enough phone lines to handle orders, and the ability to accept credit cards? Does its overall image match that of your book? Can you get your website information published?

Sometimes you must sign an exclusive distribution agreement, meaning that you won't be allowed to advertise your product in any other catalog for a set period of time, such as two years. Avoid these kinds of agreements, if possible, unless the catalog can guarantee a purchase of at least five thousand books.

Publisher Claire Kirch, formerly of the publishing firm Spinsters Ink. in Denver, Colorado, likens finding the right catalog for the book to finding a job.

"If you fit the job description, you're hired! I always look at the catalog to make sure our books are right for it," she said, adding that the book *Mother Journeys*, a collection of essays, has done very well in women's catalogs.

Once you've found the right catalog, you'll need to contact the person who chooses the merchandise and write to him or her. You can usually get the contact name, title, and catalog address by simply calling the catalog's 800 number and asking, said Rebecca Austin, a book publisher rep.

If you feel that you'd like some support in choosing and contacting the different catalog companies, consultants like Austin are willing to do the legwork. "We do basically the same thing a publisher has to do," she explains, "except we have people whom we've been working with for a long time (such as the *Signals and Wireless* catalogs). We know what they're looking for, and we can target a book better."

Lead Times

Just like everything else in the book industry, catalogs have extremely long lead times. Catalog buyers typically begin looking at Christmas products, for example, right after the holidays wrap up and make their decision of what products to list in February, March, and April. Generally, a catalog-buying committee will finalize its product selection about nine to ten months before the catalog comes out.

They may ask you to ship inventory five months before the catalog's publication date. Try to find out when the selection committee meets and time your query letter to arrive a few weeks beforehand.

Getting in Touch

Once you find a catalog that fits your book, you'll need to write a query letter (using the buyer's name and title), which is accompanied by a flyer about your book. The biggest mistake publishers make, Storey said, is simply shipping off their catalog of books with a cover letter and expecting the buyer to thumb through and pick out a few books. It isn't going to happen. The catalog will get tossed.

Essentially, you, the publisher, need to do the thinking for the buyer. Explain in your letter exactly why your book fits in with the catalog's line of merchandise (citing specific examples of products or books in the existing line that relate to your book) and why a consumer needs it. This is where your research comes in.

Storey, for example, wanted to place a book in Crate and Barrel's catalog. As part of his research, he visited the Crate and Barrel flagship retail store in Chicago and spent enough time there to get a feel for its style.

"We decided to propose a book called *Picnic*, a simple cookbook nicely done," he said. "When we made our proposal, we gave them a very specific idea that they could plug into: merchandise the book along with a picnic basket."

Crate and Barrel accepted *Picnic*, marketed it as Storey suggested, and sold more than seventy-five thousand copies.

Mention in your letter whether your book has any movie interest, audio rights, or foreign rights sales interest: anything that shows other people think it's an invaluable book to own. Include feature stories on the book, great reviews, and any articles, particularly those in special-interest magazines that show the book appeals to the catalog's specific audience.

Along with your query letter, send a flyer with general introductory information such as the title, retail price, a picture of the cover, the book size, number of illustrations, number of pages, the ISBN, and wonderful things people have said about your book. Do not send a book, at least not initially. It will likely get tossed. If your budget allows, however, send a separate photo of your book or the book cover itself.

Stella Otto, who publishes a series of backyard gardening books, conveys her book information in a clever promotional piece that she gets printed at the same time her books are produced.

On one side is the cover and on the other are the table of contents, the date the book was printed, and various promotional and review blurbs. With this, she mails a flyer with comprehensive factual information.

Once you send a query, follow up with a phone call and ask whether the buyer has any questions or requires additional information. If the catalog buyer shows interest, be prepared to send a book or two, plus a fact sheet that includes the title, retail price, shipping weight, your discount schedule, order address, order phone number, and the number of books held in stock. This last piece of information is to reassure the buyer that you'll be able to fill orders. You may want to add a notice that orders in excess of five thousand books (or whatever) require a four-week notice.

If the buyer rejects your book, try again and keep trying. Update your query letters with any new publicity or good news about the book or news clips that show the topic is now hot among the buying public.

DISCOUNTS

For the catalog business, you'll have to make up a discount schedule based on quantity ordered. Legally, you cannot give one catalog a 70 percent discount for five thousand books and a 50 percent discount to another. You must be consistent based on the quantity ordered.

You can base the schedule on the number of gross books ordered (one gross equals 144) because catalogs typically order that way or by the number of cartons of books packaged. Most publishers establish a range of a 50 percent discount for a dozen books, up to 65 percent for ten thousand books or more.

A word of caution: make it clear that the higher discount is for one order only—not orders given over six months. Some publishers, to preclude haggling, just establish a standard 50 percent discount with a footnote: for quantities larger than five hundred, please call.

You'll find that some catalogs try to impose their own terms on the publisher, asking for discounts of up to 80 percent. Don't consider it, because you won't make money. If their terms are only slightly different from yours, go with them. Otherwise, stick to your discount schedule.

Remember that catalog buyers are not lured into buying books by an offer of a deep discount but rather by the idea that the book is a "hidden gem" that will ring up thousands of sales, Storey said.

Getting Exposure at Trade Shows

A wonderful way to get noticed by catalogs is to attend trade shows that exhibit products related to your book. Each market has its own trade shows, and buyers are always looking for new items.

First, find the catalogs that match the personality of specific books you want to place. Then introduce yourself and your book, give them your business card and a flyer on your book, and be ready to explain why you think your specific book is good for that particular catalog. When you return home, call the people you've met, asking them whether they need any more information, and then send a query letter.

Shipping Terms

Catalogs usually buy books in bulk since they are considered a low-end item. Typically, they ask you to ship your books months in advance. Demand with catalogs can be volatile. Keep enough stock on hand and make sure your printer can turn an order around within a few weeks.

If your book is quite expensive, the catalog may ask you to drop-ship it. In that case, the catalog will notify you of an order for your book and a cancellation date if your book is not delivered in time. Typically, you must fill the order immediately or within an agreed-upon period of time, such as four weeks. Obviously, that means you must keep sufficient stock on hand. Expect to abide by the cataloger's shipping methods.

Payment and Returns

Most catalogs pay net thirty days. On the first order, it's wise to ask for a prepayment. If you don't know the catalog's financial reputation, ask it to fill out a credit form. You'll find out quickly whether there's a problem.

"People won't come out and say there is a problem with this guy paying on time," said publisher Stella Otto. "But they'll be real slow to respond to you. You have to read between the lines."

It's also wise to insist on a policy of no returns. This policy forces catalogs to make wise purchasing decisions in the first place rather than overbuy and leave you eating the returns nine months later.

Other Hints

Sometimes your book might be priced too low to justify the space it will take up in the catalog, said Charles Leocha, president of World Leisure Corporation. Leocha's books, *Getting to Know You* and *Getting to Know Kids in Your Life*, each sell for $6.95, too low to capture a catalog's interest.

"When a catalog gives space to a book, they'd like to get more money for each book sold," Leocha said. "If they have a choice between my book at $7 or someone else's at $14.95 and they could sell the same number of copies, they'll go with the more expensive book."

The Direct Marketing Association, with more than seventy-five years of experience in direct mail, offers a variety of services to its thirty-six hundred members. Even if you don't want to join, they might be able to point you to a myriad of resources.

Catalog Sales

Check out direct marketing magazines for two reasons. First, you must familiarize yourself with the catalog market. Second, you'll want to mail the magazine a press release about your book. For a sample issue, look online or ask for them at your local library. Some magazines offer free subscriptions to qualified subscribers. Be sure to ask about it.

21

DIRECT MARKETING

Books Are a Perfect Product for Direct Mail

The more tightly targeted your book is to niche markets, the easier it is to sell direct. Take Show What You Know Publishing (a division of Englefield and Associates Inc.) in Columbus, Ohio, for example. It specializes in books that help teachers prepare their classes for the proficiency tests given to students in Ohio, Florida, and Washington. The books are sold almost wholly by direct mail to the public schools in these states.

Mallery Press in Flint, Michigan, sells quilting books through quilt shops, direct to quilters via back-of-the-room sales, and through mail-order campaigns. To date, President Ami Simms has more than 283,000 copies of her firm's eight titles in print.

Elf Multimedia in Somerville, New Jersey, sold more than four thousand copies of *Pope John Paul II: An American Celebration*, a photo story of the Pope's U.S. visit, directly to readers of Catholic newspapers from mid-October through December.

"The best part was that I traded space in the newspapers for $2.50 per book sold through their ads. I had no upfront expenses other than creating and mailing the ads," said company President Loren Fisher.

Books are a perfect product for direct mail. They don't spoil, they can command a high markup, and they can be mailed at a special third-class bulk rate. Direct mail usually works very well if the book offer meets three criteria: it satisfies a concrete need, it makes clear that the reader can't get the book any other way or can't get it at such a bargain, and the pitch contains a great headline and copy.

How to Push down Costs without Sacrificing Quality

Mailing costs are important to consider. Before you design the mailing, it's well worth your time to visit the post office and ask about regulations and cost. Once a prototype of your mailing is complete, take it to the post office to be weighed. A fraction of an ounce can translate into hundreds of dollars of unnecessary postal expense, which can be averted simply by dropping a page, changing size, or using lighter-weight paper.

To minimize printing and postage expenses, publishers should use a standard-size envelope and paper size. A four-page letter, reply card, envelope, postage, stuffing, and copying cost about $1. Also, seek several printing bids and produce only a modest quantity until you're sure the offer is long term. But don't skimp on appearance. A cheap-looking package leaves an impression of a fly-by-night firm and turns off prospects.

Finding a Great List

Before you embark on a full-blown direct mail campaign, research your market so that you can describe your audience with precision to a list broker. Where do you get a good mailing list? There are a lot of list brokers out there willing to sell names to you, ranging in price from 10 cents to 80 cents a name. The more criteria you give for a name, income level, house owner, gender, occupation, etc., the more each name costs, but the better your "pull," or response, will be. The better you've researched your target market, the better you will be able to define a list that will work for you.

Here are a few mailing list sources to consider:

1. **Governmental Agencies:** Governmental agencies possess a wealth of information. They're typically willing to give you the names and addresses of government employees and agencies but not always the names and addresses of private citizens whom they serve. They include courts, registers of deeds, county clerks, state departments of transportation, and federal bankruptcy courts.

    Show What You Know Publishing sends flyers to school libraries and school districts, the biggest customers of the Ohio, Florida, and Washington proficiency test preparation book series. Free review copies of the book go to the curriculum director or building principal, as well as to teachers, but always with a follow-up phone call for an order. Their mailing list was obtained from Ohio's Department of Education, which provided an address of every school and the school's principal and superintendent.

    One tip offered by Cindi Englefield, company president: send all direct mail materials to the person who can authorize payment. "We put together one-piece mailers just loaded with information about the book and what the material covers. The printing isn't expensive. We use a quick print. We even bulk-mail it ourselves," Englefield said.

2. **Catalog Companies and Stores:** Visualize exactly the kind of customer, in every detail imaginable, who would be apt to buy your book through a catalog. Now research the catalog companies that are targeting that same customer and ask to rent or buy their list.

    If you buy a list, you can use it forever with no penalties. Rented lists can be used only once. Don't try to use a list more than once because list brokers plant tip-off names to catch offenders. However, the names of people who order your books or query for more information or a catalog are yours for the keeping, even if they were generated through a rented list.

Wally Bock sought lists from catalog companies and police-training companies that sold merchandise to police officers. When he called a company, he asked what it would cost to buy the list, as opposed to asking what they'd rent it for. "Some of these folks are relatively unsophisticated and don't know about renting," he said.

Bock recommends trying to get the best list possible from a reputable list broker, even if you have to pay a premium. Always ask when the list was last cleaned. A cleaned list has been updated for accuracy and dead addresses have been removed.

"The best of anything costs you money," he said. "If you get a good list broker, you'll get good lists presuming they're to be had. But they won't be cheap."

3. **Libraries:** If you're low on money and have tons of time, go to a metro library and cull company names from phone books that cover your targeted geographic area. It pays to make a phone call to get the right name of an individual in each firm as time permits. A mailing with individual names pulls far more strongly.

4. **Nonprofit Groups:** These groups are a wonderful resource for lists, but often you'll have to negotiate for use of the list, that is, offering their members a special discount, promising not to sell the list to anyone else, etc.

5. **Other Publishers:** If another publisher sells a book to an audience similar in profile to yours, propose sharing names of active respondents. You could also consider a co-op mailing with other publishers or manufacturers of complementary products. Here is some more good advice from Wally Bock: "To have a good partnership, you've got to have clear, common interests, a clear way to make decisions, and a real business purpose."

Writing the Direct Mail Letter

Bock credits the great response he receives from his direct mail offers to these key guidelines:

- In the headline, say specifically what benefit the book offers: "Here's what you need to potty train your child in one day: a doll, a big bag of M&Ms, and my ten-page booklet."
- The copy needs to include a story about somebody who has a problem or anxieties or fears about something that's bothering him or her. To solve the problem, this person has read the book and received very specific, marvelous benefits. This person should be similar in profile to the person who's reading the letter.
- Support the person's emotional decision with data and other kinds of anecdotal proof.
- Give consequences if the prospect doesn't take action: "If you don't get this book, your child's potty training ordeal may stretch over several months with tears and endless accidents."
- Get real people and credible organizations to echo your claims of proven results.
- Explain why this is the best deal the market has to offer in terms of price, quality, and convenience (and it should be!). Be sure to say the book is not available anywhere else, if that's true. A real disincentive to order by mail is an absurd charge for postage. There's absolutely no incentive to buy a book by mail at full price plus postage fees if the book is available at a bookstore.
- Ask the person to act now. You'll need to give the person a specific reason, whether it's free shipping, a specially discounted price, a $3 coupon on a potty seat, or a free special report on a related subject

such as "Ten easy and ultra-cheap kid projects for a rainy day."
- Offer a guarantee of satisfaction. This gives your prospect more confidence, and, statistically, few people return a product.
- Lend credibility to the offer by providing background information about yourself and your firm. People need to trust you before they send you their money.
- Repeat the book's benefit on the order form. "Yes, I want to learn exactly how to potty train my toddler in one day."
- Make it easy to order by accepting credit cards and having a toll-free number to call and a postage-free envelope.
- Mail to the same lists every two or three months. The results of a second and third mailing are often as good as those for the first mailing. When you fail to make a profit, it's time to find another list.

Finally, consider this advice from C. Richard Weylman of the Achievement Group: "Speak the prospect's language in every promotional letter and mailer that you create. This develops a sense in recipients' minds that you know them, you understand them, and you can truly identify with them. Use words that grab prospects' attention because the words are in their vocabulary and they are used on a day-to-day basis. As an example, when you're writing to doctors, use the word 'practice' not 'business.' Attorneys would respond to words such as 'precedent' and 'antecedent.' Using their words also demonstrates respect for who they are and they, in turn, will respect you more."

Test Marketing

As Harris suggested, before embarking on an expensive, full-blown campaign, test your list and your copy with two thousand to five thousand names. If you get a response of less than 1 percent or excessive "nixies" (wrong addresses), rework your copy or get a new list. Keep careful track of your costs and project your total profit. A revenue ratio of 2.2 times the money you spend should be considered minimum, said Tom and Marilyn Ross in *The Complete Guide to Self-Publishing.*

When asking for a sample, ask the mailing list broker to give every name starting with S, every nth name, or every name with the zip code from 40000 to 50000. Statistics show that half the total responses arrive within two weeks of the date your first order was received.

Tips for Success

Hand-addressed letters get opened more frequently than labeled letters. Also, boost your chances of the envelope getting opened by printing on it a statement about the book's benefit: "Open this envelope if you want to learn how to get your finances under control forever."

What offers pull the most? A letter sent first class (it gets much better treatment from the post office, yet it costs more), an offer with professional artwork, a reply card with a shaded background, longer letters (to save money, print on both sides of the paper), letters that offer special discounts for a short time, and promotional material that features artwork of the book cover. Also, colored papers offer flair without the accompanying higher printing cost for an additional color.

The better your list, the better your response. Develop a system to keep the list up-to-date. Make a separate list of those who responded to the offer for development of your own "house list" of qualified buyers, which you can then rent to others and use for small-scale, highly targeted mailings. Purge any names that haven't responded within the past year. Make all address changes and corrections immediately.

Maintain your house list diligently. To keep track of new addresses, make sure each piece of mail goes out with

"ADDRESS CORRECTION REQUESTED" below the return address. That way, the post office will place its address correction sticker on it before returning it to you. That allows you to update your database and minimize wasted postage.

Ultimately, make sure that people are treated with dignity and warmth when they call with an order.

22

GIFT AND SPECIALTY STORES

Selling in Nonbook Retail Stores

The gift and specialty store market is a wonderful place to sell books and allow your creativity to run wild. Yet, it's a complicated market to get into and requires a snappy, vibrant cover and attention-grabbing title to succeed.

But guess what? Gift stores, in general, keep the books they buy, and they usually pay within thirty days. That's far better than bookstores, which can take up to three months to pay and can return all books without impunity. Terms, though, are similar: you also receive a 50 percent discount on the books gift stores sell.

Consider also that there are two hundred thousand nonbookstore outlets in the country, ten times the number of bookstores, and they sell about half a billion dollars worth of books every year.

There are other advantages to selling in nonbook retail stores: Your books don't have to compete with thousands of titles, as they must in a bookstore. Retailers are willing to put out appealing counter displays or floor racks or may display your books with other items to inspire gift packages.

Gift book sales are also a lot less reliant on your promotional abilities. They are almost invariably an impulse buy. According to the latest study by the Book Industry Study Group, fully 33 percent of all books purchased by consumers were made as an impulse buy, oftentimes spurred by an in-store promotion.

People don't go into retail stores looking specifically for a book, said retail distributor Jim Denardo: "But once they see the book, the life that's in it, they grab it! They know! The key is getting it into stores and getting it in front of them."

Finally, retailers are less snobby about small publishers than bookstores can be. If they see a cover and title that will sell, they'll choose the book over a more staid selection from a bigger house.

Preparing your book

Before you attempt the specialty market, be sure your book has what it takes. This market, more than any other, requires an eye-catching cover. We're talking four-color, a title in bold, colorful print, and a professional-looking illustration, graphic, or photograph. (Photographs usually work best for cookbooks, although not always.) Remember that the monster publishers such as Time-Life invest heavily in both the cover and the layout of the book's interior; these books will sit side-by-side with your books, so don't lose out on the first impression.

Second, you'll need an irresistible come-hither title and subtitle, particularly for gift stores. Here are some you might have heard: *Nice Guys Don't Get Laid*; *P.S., I Love You*; *Random Acts of Kindness*; *1,001 Ways to Be Romantic*; and *365 Days of Creative Play*.

"It has been a time when emotions run higher than sales, and the books that succeed often do so not because of language and logic but because of how they make readers feel," stated a February 2009 article filed by the Associated Press and published online by CBS News. The way a book and the title of that book make readers feel are especially important for success in the gift market.

But a great title doesn't promise an easy road. After Marcus Melton, author of *Nice Guys Don't Get Laid*, decided that the Spencer Gifts chain stores would be a perfect market for his book, he realized that persistence took on a new definition.

"I sent it to the buyer they had and got no answer," he said. "I sent it again. I received a turndown. I kept making calls, twice, maybe three times. I did with other chains, too, but they were the ones who finally picked me up."

Chain stores such as Spencer Gifts, however, do have a downside. They pay only 25 to 30 percent of the retail price. For its five-thousand-book buy, Spencer's also asked Melton to provide five hundred point-of-purchase displays (POPs), which cost $2 a piece. The margin of profit was slim, Melton admitted, "but I shipped it, it was gone, I got a check, and it was over. There were no returns."

Sometimes the books in your line may be perfect for the gift market if only they had a makeover with a new cover, title, or package—or all three. Consider the possibilities. A children's book on birds could come packaged with eggs that hatch when immersed in water. A children's camping guide with a compass would make a perfect gift for a favorite niece or nephew.

The *Do It* series became a retail marketing hit partly due to the books' easily portable nature. The gardening book, for example, is bound together by a single rivet, much like paint-sample cards. Published by Chronicle Books, it was picked up by Crate and Barrel stores, numerous gift stores, and bookstores. Fueling the good publicity were two design awards and a mention in *U.S. News & World Report*. Company sales climbed to nearly $800,000, according to the article.

USING A SALES REP

If you choose sales reps to distribute your book, there are two ways to go: either with a network of independent sales reps or with a regional or national organization of sales reps.

WHICH IS BEST FOR YOU?

If your book has national appeal, consider going with a national organization of reps. The obvious advantage is you won't have to patch together a national sales force yourself. You'll have one central point for sales information, and you'll write only one commission check each month. The drawbacks are you can't talk to the individual reps and you lose significant control. There's nothing you can do if they have weak reps in specific territories because of the exclusivity agreement under which they operate.

Finding and contracting with independent sales reps is obviously messier, but it gives you much greater influence. How do you put together an effective sales force? You can find a good sales rep by calling or visiting the stores you've targeted. Ask the owner for the name of the rep who sells its best-selling gift books in the price range of your book. Even better, ask for the sales rep's name who sells merchandise related to your book. Then ask about the sales rep's reputation. When you keep hearing the same name pop up for a specific geographic area, you'll have your candidate.

To get the names of stores to call in a given geographic area, call the marketing office of a trade show and ask for its mailing list of the most recent show (these lists are often divided by size, location, and type of shop), suggests publisher Diane Pfeifer in her PMA newsletter column, "Gift Rap."

You could also ask other publishers who have published gift-market-type books—tactfully, of course—for their list of sales reps. This is a big favor, so you'll want to establish a relationship first, Pfeifer suggests. Another common way to find a sales rep is to place an ad in trade gift magazines describing your book and its potential market. Also, look for ads subtitled "Lines Wanted."

When you're ready to sign up a sales rep, ask him or her about the territory he or she reaches, the discounts he or she pays, the trade magazines he or she reads, and what criteria he or she uses for books. Ask to see the rep's catalog, how often it's published, what order quantities are, the hottest times for book sales, and lead times for catalog listings and distribution. Also, ask about the publisher's responsibilities.

Once you decide on a rep, make sure you sign an agreement that specifies his or her responsibilities, territory, commission, and markets.

How Distributors Work

Book distributors typically use a contingent of sales reps across the country to sell your books. They not only write orders for your book but also handle all shipping, billing, and collections.

Typically, distributors send out seasonal catalogs to retail buyers. They may display their wares at major gift shows or a permanent showroom, use road reps, and/or promote your book to the media. Each distributor's terms vary; there really is no industry standard. Research carefully the different terms each offers and ask about more favorable discounts depending on volume. Discounts may vary from 55 to 68 percent. A distributor may also charge for freight and various fees, such as putting your book in its catalog.

How do you find a distributor that is right for you? Look at the books in each distributor's catalog that best match your line. Sourcebooks, for example, chooses books that "lighten up lives," whether it's humor, inspirational, or spiritual, according to Michael Ritter, a former sales manager.

"We don't want a collection of quotes or sayings but books that have a little more meat to them, where you can spend a lot of time reading them but you don't have to read them cover to cover," said Ritter, adding that the firm rejects about 99 percent of the unsolicited book pitches it receives.

Dot Gibson, president of Dot Gibson Distributors, looks for books with an excellent cover, name, layout, and quality of printing, and it also looks for cookbooks and good recipes.

Gibson said her firm generally buys about one hundred books at a time and immediately pays the publisher. Other gift book distributors don't pay the publisher until after the books are sold. Your contract should spell out the timing of payment, shipping turnaround times, discounts, book return credits, etc.

A distributor or sales rep may ask for a point-of-purchase display to enhance sales. Many publishers have found that a sturdy, highly visual display is a good investment and will pay off in sales.

If possible, put four titles on a display instead of one because you'll get four times the opportunity to make a sale.

Trade Shows

There is no better place to get acquainted with the movers and shakers of the industry than trade shows. You'll meet people from every area of involvement: media, suppliers, distributors, manufacturers, and those hard-to-get-to buyers. Ask for business cards (to use later in a mailing list) and solicit comments about your books. You may want to get feedback from distributors about book ideas, and they may offer to take on your title.

You'll make a ton of contacts in the space of a few hours—contacts to immediately pursue when you return home. Seminars at the trade shows can also be of immense help. You'll get free advice and sometimes direct help with a given problem.

A trade show is a spectacular place to check out the lines of sales rep groups or distributors to find a good fit between your books and their products. Or they may check out your book line and approach you! This is also a good place to talk to store owners and ask for their recommendations for a rep.

If your books are regional or niche, consider displaying them at smaller trade shows. If your line has national appeal, choose the larger shows.

In general, winter and summer shows are best. In winter, shops are looking for resort, souvenir, and catalog products. In summer, they're shopping for the holidays. You'll get weaker results in fall and spring shows.

Before committing to a display booth, call the show office and ask for the names and phone numbers of previous exhibitors. Call a few of them and ask for their results and for any tips for a successful day.

Other Pointers

Pfeifer and other publishers suggest these tried-and-true strategies:

- Send a direct mail piece to wholesale gift shops. A good mailing list is pivotal; you may want to get together with other publishers to share names. The best list would include only names of vendors who have consistently responded to mailings.
- When you design the display that will hold the books (six to twelve is a good range), make sure you print on the back of the display the following: "To reorder NAME OF BOOK, call (800) XXX-XXXX or visit us on the web at XXXXX.com."
- Think about how your book could tie in with an existing product. Have you published a book on potty training? Call up a potty chair manufacturer and propose pairing your products. Your idea will be far better accepted if you present prototype art for the packaging.
- Strongly consider joining trade or professional associations, such as the Hobby Industry Association or the National Craft Association. These associations are clearinghouses for news on seminars, trade shows, meetings, and networking opportunities. They sometimes offer services, too, such as market research and marketing.
- If your book line is too small to get entrance into a trade show, offer to rep a friend's gift line.

23

Alternative Sales Platforms

Corporations, Associations, Foundations, and the Government

Corporate Sales

When Proctor and Gamble offered a three-book set of Curious George books to spur sales of Luvs and Pampers diapers, Charmin toilet paper, and Puffs tissues, the campaign was enormously successful, both for P&G and the publisher. Customers bought more than thirty thousand copies at a cost of $4.99 and proof-of-purchase seals from ninety thousand P&G products.

The corporate incentive market is huge; estimates range around $20 billion. Books capture an estimated 6 percent, or $1.5 billion, of the market. And once a corporation buys your books, it keeps your books.

For small orders of up to five thousand, corporations generally take a respectable discount of 50–55 percent. As the size of order goes up, the profit per book goes down. For large orders of twenty thousand to twenty-five thousand, for example, a corporation may take up to a 70 percent discount or pay a dollar or two above printing cost. Yet compared to a national distributor, which has the privilege of returning any or all books without penalty, it's still a good deal. Corporations also pay a lot more quickly than book distributors.

Sometimes a corporation gives away gifts for the public relations value. Gifts may go to an employee or a vendor at Christmastime or to celebrate an anniversary or as a thank-you for a loyal client. Every time recipients look at the book, it is hoped, they will think fondly of the company. The most common use of book incentives right now is tying a travel guide into vacation packages, said former Incentive editor Jennifer Juergens.

A Mexican cookbook, for example, was used to promote an employee incentive trip to Cancun. The cover detailed the trip's highlights, whetting the employees' appetite not only for Mexican food but also for a delicious vacation.

Books are a chosen premium for many corporations because they're inexpensive to buy, are easy to ship, and have a high perceived value because they educate and entertain. A book enriches the life of a person who receives it, making it a much better gift than a T-shirt tucked away in a drawer. People typically keep books around a long time, so they stay as an eternal reminder of a special corporate program, event, competition, or trip. Books are also easy to customize with a new cover, discount coupons in the back of the book, stickers, or an inserted letter. They can also be easily packaged to complement the company's product.

Despite these advantages and the market potential, small publishers often fail to think of selling to corporations or hesitate to do so because the process seems too daunting. In all honesty, selling books to corporations can involve a hefty investment of time. A publisher needs to research the various corporations, hound the corporations for a decision, and perhaps travel to the corporate sites for negotiations. There have been cases, however, when a sale has taken only one phone call and a follow-up visit.

Research is pivotal when trying to target the corporation. Sometimes it's obvious. If you've written a book *Crock-Pot Recipes to Die For*, you'll want to pitch companies that sell Crock-Pots.

Books that involve text on a particular product are the easiest to sell. Some require greater creativity to dream up a connection to a corporation. Have you written a book on a famous basketball player, for example? Contact sporting goods and tennis shoe companies. A book on saving energy might go to an insulation firm or to an electric company trying to get customers to agree to an energy-saving device. Child care books are frequent giveaways of parenting magazines.

To be considered by a corporation, send a copy of your book and a letter. Your letter should:

- Stress the relevance of your book to the corporation or product.
- Give proof in your letter that your book is a winner. Use sales statistics, testimonials, book reviews, etc.
- Educate the company as to the advantages of using a book as a premium as well as the lasting value of a book, how people will appreciate the content, the ease of customizing the book, and the simplicity of shipping.

Some have suggested thinking ahead and listing companies in the book, where relevant, in order to be more favorably regarded by them for a premium sale. This tactic can sometimes backfire; you may inadvertently mention a loathsome competitor or end up with a chintzy-looking book.

After you send your book and letter to the appropriate brand manger, make follow-up phone calls and don't give up. Be prepared to answer their objections.

Lori Marcus of Cadillac Press in Lake Tahoe had good luck pitching her book, *Bartending Inside-Out*. A company agreed to pay a 50 percent discount for the $14.95 book. A small sale, maybe, but it entirely paid for Marcus's first printing of two thousand books.

Negotiation is often a big part of corporate sales. Marcus agreed to insert a premium liquor name every time a recipe called for it and to customize the cover. The company, in turn, agreed to pay for the special color and the text changes. Her negotiation illustrates a point: closely work with your printer for estimates when negotiating a deal.

Marcus considers herself a beginner but admits she did compose a "strong, strong query letter." She says, "Two of the people called me while they were reading the letter. I wrote that most liquor companies give away T-shirts and gadgets. Why not give away knowledge? And that's what got them."

Marcus not only captured a book deal but also was hired by Seagram's to conduct an employee seminar. She then pitched her book to liquor distributors (the salespeople want copies so they know what they're talking about), hotel chains, and restaurant supply firms.

"These sales take a long, long time," Marcus said. "You have to be prepared to wait. There are so many different people they have to go through, and they'll forget about it if you let them. I must have made thousands of phone calls."

Eventually, she was able to put together a deal with Allied Domecq, who bought books to give away to all the managers from the Bennigan's chain. Currently, *Bartending Inside-Out* is being used by six different bartending/hospitality schools as a textbook.

To locate a specific corporation, we suggest seeing firsthand what's out there. Get in your car and drive to a large store in a metro area to familiarize yourself with the products (you will need this information in customizing your letter to each company). As you do your research, seek out specific information on the corporation with these two questions in mind: (1) Why would your product appeal to this organization? and (2) Do the product and your book appeal to the same kind of target audience (upscale, downscale, relevant to the book's subject matter)? Your final step is to call the company to identify the contact name, usually the marketing manager or brand manager.

Besides helping you identify exactly who should receive your package, a phone call affords you the opportunity to introduce yourself and your book and sets up the expectation for its arrival. About seven business days after shipping, make a follow-up call.

TIPS:

- Ask for half the payment prior to getting the book printed and the remainder within thirty days of delivery.
- When a corporation asks for more information, be prepared and make a good impression.
- Chat with the marketing manager and find out what he or she might have in mind. Then, professionally prepare a customized mock-up and deliver, pronto!
- Visit trade shows and conventions to meet personally with potential corporate buyers. For a directory of trade shows, go to a metro library and consult Trade Shows Worldwide, published by Gale Research. If that's not possible, call a few companies and ask the marketing secretary for the major trade shows.
- Speaking of trade shows, go to those geared for incentive/premium buyers. The largest, by far, is called the Motivation Show, an annual event attended by about twenty-two thousand people each year. It's held at McCormick Place in Chicago alternately in September and October. Anyone is welcome, and there's no fee for entry if you register ahead of time.
- Contact the Incentive Manufacturers Representatives Association (IMRA) Inc. This association is made up of manufacturers and sales reps in the incentive industry. It's possible that a sales rep (who undoubtedly has more contacts than most publishers) may be willing to pick up your book and sell it to a corporation for a commission of 5 to 10 percent.

Corporations Use Books!

Here is a list of corporations that have used books as effective promotional tools for history, premium, incentive, and product sales.

Avon	Diary
Coca-Cola	Coca-Cola girls advertising and art history book
Coors Beer	Colorado scenic calendar as distributor gifts
Crate and Barrel	Grilling cookbook in picnic basket
Deere and Company	Company history
National Arbor Day Foundation	Tree care guidebook with membership
Quaker Oats	*Gone with the Grits* cookbook offer
Victoria's Secret	Romance novels

Associations

You can also make a bundle selling to associations, but the process is not as straightforward.

Your first trip must be to the library, where you'll find the *Encyclopedia of Associations*, published by Gale Research. Here you'll find a huge range of associations; the membership count, contact information, and budget; and whether the association publishes a newsletter.

Use this information when trying to figure out your pitch to the association. In your letter, you'll need to detail how your book relates to the association's mission and philosophy. For smaller associations (memberships of fewer than one hundred thousand), seek out no more than a review. Many publishers run an ad alongside the review to reinforce the review and to provide ordering information.

For advice on querying a large association, which represents a potentially huge sale, we talked to Bev Harris, one of the rare consultants in the country who specializes in these kinds of sales.

"Most [associations] are nonprofit, so here's your angle: they usually publish a newsletter that they direct mail to members. Propose to them that your book will help fund-raise for them, and propose this deal: they agree to review your book in their members' newsletter, and they also include an order form for the book right in the newsletter itself. You supply the information (and mini sales pitch) that you want on the order form. Some publishers provide the actual artwork so they can ensure that the form will look good. The association gets 50 percent of the retail price (or 40 percent, or 25 percent, depending on how low you think they'll go). You get the rest. The offer charges members full price plus shipping/handling.

"You and the publisher agree which newsletter will contain the review. Usually, for accounting checks and balances, one person takes the money and the other fulfills the order. But, I have set up huge deals where the association trusted me to handle both sides and printed my address and ordering number on the form."

This is a great way, by the way, to line up cash coming in before your printing bills hit. You can expect a 4 to 10 percent response rate, depending on how strong the endorsement is. If you know a person at the association, especially a bigwig, you can sandwich in a powerful endorsement to pump up response rates.

Harris said association negotiations are a delicate art. A woman, for example, sent her this query:

"I started to write a proposal letter but got the squirmy feeling that asking for a review in exchange for a kickback on the book was kind of unethical. Don't get me wrong; I'll do it in a heartbeat—I am just worried that the associations that I approach may be instantly turned off. Have you run into this? Or are they quite receptive? Have you ever furnished them with a review that they can edit as they see fit?"

Harris responded with the following note:

"When you have a squirmy feeling and you're trying to sell someone on an idea, listen to that squirmy feeling. Keep thinking your approach through until it 'feels' right. Here's how I make it feel right.

"First, I read everything I can get my hands on and talk to someone who's involved, to get a feel for the association. I want to know what they are excited about. I want to know their issues and who's who. That's the 'Abe Lincoln approach.' Abe said, 'If I had nine hours to chop down a tree, I'd spend six hours sharpening my ax.' The reason you feel squirmy is because your ax isn't sharp enough. The bigger the tree, the sharper your ax needs to be.

"Here's an example of how I set up a deal with one particular nonprofit association. The book I was promoting was one by a popular columnist, and the deal that we ended up with was worth about $100,000 in publisher profits. (It was a really big tree.) First, I did an Internet search and found they had a large website. I printed off about one hundred pages. They included their mission statement, the complete archive of their newsletters, and I used a highlighter as I read.

"Make an appointment with someone who's a decision maker. If you're a writer, invent a reason to write about them (something that's in their best interests) and actually follow through and do it. That gives you the ideal reason to make an appointment with a biggie. A telephone appointments can work just fine.

"Because this particular nonprofit had 600,000 members, I invested $750 in a visit to Washington, D.C., where I met with an official at the organization. I'm sure he wondered why he was spending the time with me. During that meeting I basically just asked him what was important to him about his nonprofit and found out what else he was personally interested in.

Alternative Sales Platforms

"I said I'd like to help the nonprofit by doing something to encourage people to join or to help in fund-raising. I asked him what types of things they do, because it would help me think of ideas.

"He suggested a bunch of things (that I couldn't help with). I thanked him for so many interesting ideas. I also followed up by finding a way to use the book to help him personally with a project he was working on. The ol' Zig Zigler idea: help other people get what they want and then they'll help you get what you want.

"Still, everything I did was just being helpful. I followed through on the small things I had promised, and three weeks later, this man called me to thank me. Timing is everything. That's when I asked him whom I could talk to about getting a book review for fund-raising. He not only gave me the name of the president, but he called the man and told him he thought I had a good idea. Then I called the president and, again, asked him his ideas on how I could help fund-raise. I listened carefully and then proposed the deal.

"He didn't ask me to, but I arranged for a slip to be added to a mailing I was doing, inviting folks to contribute $25 toward a membership to the nonprofit. Just being genuinely nice. And at the same time thinking, 'Maybe next summer when we come out in trade paperback, I can repeat this deal.'

"Everything was done in person and on the telephone until the last step, when I arranged for a simple 'letter of agreement' (not 'contract'). The result: an enthusiastic endorsement, 10,000 books at $24.95 each, and our cut 50 percent. Note that associations often don't use the bookseller's lingo 'discount.' You start by telling them the retail price and tell them they get such-and-such percent for each book sold.

"The idea is you feel comfortable when you know you are helping them. Most folks just say, 'Will you do this for me?' You start with finding out about them. In today's high-tech society, we're still the same. We like people who are nice.

"I'd want to know, before writing any letters, what the mission of the association is, what their current 'wants' are. Try asking this question: If you could wave a magic wand on behalf of your organization, what would you ask for? You'll be surprised at the answer.

"Are they trying to get more members? Outlaw cruelty to horses? Set up a successful horse show? Expect a surprise when you ask that question.

"Taking the horse example, suppose your contact is currently stressed about how to get more people to attend a horse show. You think, 'How could I help?' Well, if they'd send you some flyers, you could tuck one in each book and add them into your mailings. Surprise! You could post on some newsgroups to announce the show. Then tell them that you did that for them.

"While you are doing all these nice things, you will probably realize that they might be willing to put a stack of your brochures by the door at the horse show or even stuff programs with your order forms. By figuring out how to help them, you think of new ways to help yourself! Now you've got a contact, who turns into a friend, who helps you get that book review, suggests other places for you to promote your book, even introduces you to contacts at new places!

"If the association is too small to invest time 'just being nice,' find smaller ways to be nice. But take the time to study up on what they're all about before you contact anyone and find a reason for the contact that serves them more than you and you'll find that queasy feeling disappears. All of a sudden, you've got genuine excitement."

Government Agencies

Just like corporations, the government spends billions of dollars in supplies and services, and it does indeed buy a lot of books. Training guides are particularly hot with the government, said Michael Keating, former research manager for the publications *Government Product News*, *Government Procurement*, and *Government Marketing Newsletter*, as well as author of the book *Introduction to the Government Market*.

"A major Midwest city just spent $60,000 on diversity training and study guides to help city employees work more cooperatively," he said.

At a workshop, Keating told a Santa Fe author who published a book on how to create and update a web page that she will probably find government agencies a very lucrative market since many government employees are struggling with this very problem.

"By all means, there are opportunities. Some people say there's more red tape selling to the government, but it's like selling to any large organization, be it General Motors or whatever. And there are advantages, such as 'set-asides' [vendor preferences] for women and minorities."

Keating said that the Internet is a wonderful place to find what's called "request for quotes." Basically, a government calls for bids for certain products. There are also for-profit services on the Internet that will notify vendors when the government puts out a quote for their specific products.

Foundations

A foundation is generally defined as a nongovernmental nonprofit organization with its own funds and program, managed by its own trustees and directors. Matching your book with the appropriate foundation is another excellent way to reach a wide audience and garner large-quantity sales. There are currently more than twenty thousand foundations in the United States, and there is one out there to advance virtually any cause or ideology that could be imagined.

What better place to search for a niche market for your book than within the foundation arena; it is a venue with as many different purposes, theories, and goals as there are books themselves.

Foundations can be broken down into several major categories, including independent foundations, company-sponsored foundations, community foundations, and public charities. The key is finding the foundation whose mission matches the subject matter and the objective of your particular book. A few salient examples can be found from within Jenkins Group's own client base.

Dr. Burton Folsom had written a highly readable historical account of Michigan's early entrepreneurs called *Empire Builders*. These people helped lead the United States to global prominence in cars, chemicals, and cornflakes. As Dr. Folsom explained, they all "shared a stubborn persistence to invent and market something that would make life simpler for millions of people."

With the highlighting of Michigan's entrepreneurial history and spirit as the mission statement of this title, it stands to reason that one should look for a foundation that shares this mission, which is exactly what Jenkins Group did.

Jenkins Group matched *Empire Builders* with the Edward Lowe Foundation, a Michigan-based organization that advertises its purpose as one of championing "the entrepreneurial spirit by providing information research and education experiences which support second stage entrepreneurs and the free enterprise system." The Lowe Foundation bought twelve hundred copies of Folsom's book to give to high school students around the state of Michigan.

In much the same way, Sharon Olson was able to sell five thousand copies of her book, *Your Gift*, on illness and the end of life to a foundation whose objective meshed nicely with the subject matter and sentiment of her work. The Roxane Pain Institute, a foundation supported by Roxane Laboratories and a large supporter of hospice, used *Your Gift* as a premium/gift item to hospice volunteers attending a national conference.

If you are not familiar with foundations that may have objectives similar to those of your book, a good way to get started looking for the perfect match is with the Foundation Center (fdncenter.org).

Conclusion

The Four Ps Revisited

So, we've given you the tools and advice to build your book business. Those four Ps can carry you a long way on your publishing path and will make the process that much simpler (thanks, Mr. McCarthy!). Custom book publishing is all about taking the steps needed to create, promote, and place the book you've always wanted and the book that everyone else is going to enjoy.

Start your venture by investing in professional people and services to create the best product possible. During editorial, design, printing, and marketing, it's always best to have a pro in your back pocket. You may have the final say, but listen to those more experienced folks around you and see where collaboration can take you. Remember to do your research so you can price your book right for your particular market (and so that you'll turn a profit). You'll have to work hard to get your book placed where readers will see it, like it, and buy it, which means tirelessly promoting your book early on, in person, online, and in stores.

Finally (here comes another P), always be proactive. If there is anything we can learn from the changes in the publishing industry, it's that those who take action and adapt will prosper. You have the information and resources to create a successful book and a profitable business. Now go out there and make us proud. Best of luck to you.

Appendix

Checklists

Here are some handy checklists to make sure you're hitting all the basics for interior and exterior trade standards.

Front Cover

- Title
- Subtitle
- Author's name
- Foreword by (if applicable)
- Testimonial (optional)
- Series Name (if applicable)

Spine

- Author's name
- Title
- Publishing company logo or name

Back Cover / Flaps

- **Back Cover Headline:** A compelling headline is key to helping your potential buyer relate to your book. Do not simply repeat your title here. Find your "hook."
- **Marketing Copy:** (Approx. 250 words). Good sales copy answers the following questions: 1. What is the book about? 2. Why should the

buyer purchase your book? Get to the point as quickly and as efficiently as possible. Often, this is all the potential buyer will read before making a buying decision. 3. What are the promises and benefits? 3. What does the book provide the reader? Better health, wealth, entertainment, or a better life, etc.? Think about whom you are talking to and what they are going to take away from the book.

- **Testimonials and Endorsements:** It is a great idea to have testimonials on your book. You should request these from experts in the field you are writing about. Be sure to allow enough time for your reviewers to read the book and write the testimonial. Typically, most would like four to six weeks.

- **Author Bio:** (Approx. 75–100 words). Provide a short biography about yourself to show that you are the decisive authority on your topic.

- **Author Photo:** A photo submitted as a 300-dpi-resolution file (5" × 7") will be of sufficient quality for appropriate sizing on the back / flap. We strongly recommend getting a professional photo taken for this purpose. Tell the photographer what you intend to do with the photo, as there may be permission paperwork you need to sign to use the photo on your book.

- **Category:** This is generally placed on the top inside of the front flap on a hardcover book and on the top or bottom of the back cover of a softcover book. Listing the proper category will ensure that your book is properly placed on bookstore shelves and will be easy to find. To determine what category your book should be in, you can look up similar books on Amazon.com and see what types of categories they fall into.

Appendix

- **Publisher Information:** Book Publishing Company Name, City, State should be placed on the back cover.
- **Copyright Notice:** © 20XX Author Name should appear on the back cover of the book.
- **Price:** Your price is determined by your sales goals and investment in the book. You should carefully evaluate your return on investment based on what you've spent to create the book and how much you need to make on each book to make a profit. You should also look at books similar to yours at the bookstore to see where the competition is priced. This is generally placed on the top inside of the front flap on the dust jacket of a hardcover book and on the top or bottom of the back cover of a softcover or casebound book.
- **Barcode:** A barcode with your International Standard Book Number (ISBN) and price will be placed on the back cover. The barcode is essential for commercial sales of your book.
- **NOTE:** If the book is printed in a foreign country, it also must also have a statement of manufacture. This allows the books to pass through customs. Without the statement, the books are liable to be held indefinitely in customs. The statement may read as below: Printed in Singapore

Interior

- Front matter order is correct: half title page, full title page, copyright, dedication, contents, foreword, preface, acknowledgments, introduction
- Front matter is numbered in Roman, not Arabic
- Make sure it isn't "Table of Contents," just "Contents"

- "Acknowledgments" and "Foreword" are spelled correctly
- Chapter names in "Contents" match chapter heads and running heads
- Chapter page numbers are correct in "Contents"
- Drop caps are checked and consistent; if drop caps aren't used, check the first line treatment on each chapter head to insure consistency
- Pull quotes are checked and consistent
- Widows/orphans are noted
- The flow of words from page to page is correct
- Page numbers are correct and consistently placed per the book design
- Words are not broken from page to page
- Capitalization of titles is correct according to CMS
- A-heads, B-heads, and such are consistent; if title caps are used, check all
- Em dash use is consistent and correct
- Use of hyphens is consistent and correct
- Index numbers are correct (if applicable)

If you have any questions about these checklist elements, feel free to contact Jenkins Group at (800) 644-0133.

Bibliography

Alan, Canton. "Don't Publish Crap, Don't Buy Crap." A Saturday Rant (blog), April 9, 2005. http://asaturdayrant.blogspot.com/2005/04/dont-publish-crap-dont-buy-crap.html.

Bringhurst, Robert. *The Elements of Typographic Style*. Vol. 3.1. Vancouver, BC: Hartley & Marks, 2005.

Cole, David. *The Complete Guide to Book Marketing*. New York, NY: Allworth Press, 2004.

Daye, Stephen. *The Oath of the Freeman*. Philadelphia, PA: Press of the Woolly Whale, 1939.

Epstein, Jason. *Book Business* New York, NY: W. W. Norton & Company, 2002.

Fitzgerald, F. Scott. *The Great Gatsby*. New York, NY: Scribner, 1999.

Gallagher, Dan. T*he Pleistocene Redemption*. Brooksville, FL: Ancient Prophecies Press, 1998.

Gerritsen, Tess. Tess Gerritsen Blog (blog). http://www.tessgerritsen.com/blog (accessed 2011).

Glazer, Sarah. "How to Be Your Own Publisher." *The New York Times*, April 24, 2005.

Grothe, Dr. Mardy. *Oxymoronica*. New York, NY: Harper, 2004.

Heiltzer, Mel, and Mark Shatz. *Comedy Writing Secrets*. Cincinnati, OH: Writer's Digest Books, 2005.

IndieBound. http://www.indiebound.org/ (accessed 2011).

"IndieBound: BookSense Evolved." American Booksellers Association. http://www.bookweb.org/booksense.html (accessed 2011).

Italie, Hillel. "A Tough Year for Reading." CBS News, February 11, 2009.

Jenkins, Jerrold. *The Insider's Guide to Large Quantity Book Sales*. Traverse City, MI: Jenkins Group Inc., 2005.

Jones, Margaret. "Mergers-and-Acquisitions Aftershocks." *Publisher's Weekly*, September 20, 1999.

Karasik, Paul. *How to Make It Big in the Seminar Business*. New York, NY: McGraw-Hill, 2004.

McLaughlin, Robert. "Oppositional Aesthetics/Oppositional I deologies: A Brief Cultural History of Alternative Publishing in the U.S." *LitLine*, 1995.

McPherson & Company. https://www.mcphersonco.com/cs.php?f[0]=frd&fNM=na.php&naNUM=partners (accessed 2011).

National Book Critic's Circle. http://www.bookcritics.org (accessed 2011).

Perrin, Noel, and Michael McCurdy. *Third Person Rural: Further Essays of a Sometime Farmer*. Boston, MA: David R. Godine Publisher, 1999.

Pfeifer, Diane. PMA Forum Online. http://www.pma-online.org (accessed 2011).

Plimpton, George. *The Writer's Chapbook: A Compendium of Fact, Opinion, Wit, and Advice from the Twentieth Century's Preeminent Writers*. New York, NY: Modern Library, 1999.

Bibliography

Poynter, Dan. "Book Industry Statistics." Para Publishing. 2008. http://www.parapublishing.com/sites/para/resources/statistics.cfm (accessed 2011).

Prisciotta, Daniel A. *Defend Your Wealth: Protecting Your Assests in an Increasingly Volatile World*. Ramsey, NJ: Prisco Publishing, 2011.

R.R. Bowker, LLC. 2011. http://www.bowker.com/ (accessed 2011).

Sabah, Joe. "How to Create Book and Speech Titles That Sizzle and Sell." Money Making Secrets. http://www.joesabah.com/ (accessed 2011).

Sutherland, John. "John Sutherland is shocked by the state of book-reviewing on the web." *The Telegraph*, November 19, 2006.

Ugresic, Dubravka, Celia Hawkesworth, and Damion Searls. *Thank You for Not Reading*. Champaign, IL: Dalkey Archive, 2003.

Wallace, Sean. "Publishing in the future: the potential and reality of POD." *Locus Online*, March 10, 2004.

Warren, Lissa. *The Savvy Author's Guide to Book Publicity*. New York, NY: Da Capo Press, 2004.

Weylman, Richard C. "Direct Mail That Gets Opened and Read." *SOHO Marketing*, 2000.

White, E.B. *The Elements of Style*. New York, NY: Longman, 1999.

Woll, Tom. *Publishing for Profit*. Chicago, IL: Chicago Review Press, 2010.

About the Author

Jerrold R. Jenkins

A graduate of Alma College and a lifelong Michigander, Jerrold R. Jenkins worked as a financial and investment management group account executive before founding Jenkins Group in 1988 as Publisher's Design Service and Publisher's Distribution Service. In 1994, he sold his interest in Publisher's Distribution Service, retaining his interest and position as owner and president of Publisher's Design Service. In 1995, the corporate name became Jenkins Group Inc. New staff came on board, and the company purchased *SmallPress* magazine, now known as *Independent Publisher*. At that time, Jerrold also began two publishing imprints, Rhodes and Easton, under which he coauthored and published *Publish to Win!* and *Inside the Bestsellers,* and Sage Creek Press. It was while working with these imprints that the idea of expanding his company to embrace custom book publishing was born.

Today, Jenkins Group specializes in three areas: custom book publishing, finely tuned postpublication book marketing and distribution services, and a highly regarded book awards program that includes the Axiom Business Book Awards, the eLit Awards, the Independent Publisher (IPPY) Book Awards, the Living Now Book Awards, and the Moonbeam Children's Book Awards.

As CEO, Jerrold's role today is twofold: he consistently creates new products and services to best serve the ever-evolving publishing industry and he continues to work with corporate and entrepreneurial clients and as a consultant to publishers, speaking throughout the country on the benefits of custom book publishing and the marketing opportunities that abound.

Jerrold is married and has four children.

The Independent Publisher

Composed in Minion Pro with display lines in Sabon Roman

Minion Pro *is an Adobe Original typeface designed by Robert Slimbach. The first version of Minion was released in 1990. Cyrillic additions were released in 1992, and finally the OpenType Pro version was released in 2000. Minion Pro is inspired by classical, old style typefaces of the late Renaissance, a period of elegant, beautiful, and highly readable type designs. Minion Pro combines the aesthetic and functional qualities that make text type highly readable with the versatility of OpenType digital technology, yielding unprecedented flexibility and typographic control.*

Sabon Roman *was designed by Jan Tschichold in 1967. In the early 1960s, the German masterprinters' association requested that a new typeface be designed and produced in identical form on both Linotype and Monotype machines so that text and technical composition would match. Walter Cunz at Stempel responded by commissioning Jan Tschichold to design the most faithful version of Claude Garamond's serene and classical roman yet to be cut. The boldface and particularly the italic are limited by the twin requirements of Linotype and Monotype hot metal machines. Bitstream's Cursive is a return to the form of one of Garamond's late italics, recently identified. Punches and matrices for the romans survive at the Plantin-Moretus Museum.*